Prayer

the Key to Organizing Chaos

Prayer

the Key to Organizing Chaos

Judith Gilmore Black

Tate Publishing & *Enterprises*

Prayer: the Key to Organizing Chaos

This title is also available as a Tate Out Loud product. Visit www.tatepublishing.com for more information.

Published by Tate Publishing & Enterprises, LLC
127 E. Trade Center Terrace | Mustang, Oklahoma 73064 USA
1.888.361.9473 | www.tatepublishing.com

Tate Publishing is committed to excellence in the publishing industry. The company reflects the philosophy established by the founders, based on Psalm 68:11,
"The Lord gave the word and great was the company of those who published it."

Cover design by Nathan Harmony
Interior design by Leah LeFlore

Published in the United States of America

ISBN: 978-1-60604-593-0
1. Religion 2. Application
08.10.28

Dedication

To my mom, Clara Vos Gilmore, who taught me how to be a good homemaker then modeled how Christ transforms a life.

To my dear husband, Al, whose encouragement made this book become a reality, who models Christ because his love has never failed me.

To my children who have given me endless hours of love, laughter, pride, and fulfillment.

To my grandchildren who hold my breath in their smiles, my joy in their love, my vision in their future.

To mothers and women everywhere who hold the key to homes full of joy, love, prayer, and a vision of God in everything they touch.

To God be all glory, great things He has done!

Introduction

It's hard to see God in the toilet bowl! Watching my reflection disappear with the last swirls, my number one least favorite household task, I wonder how many other women find it difficult to feel any self-worth doing this job on a daily basis. Even more difficult, I wonder, is it to find an image of God or reminders of His presence and love while working in the home. No supervisor is ever there to give you a pat on the back. There are no monetary raises or rewards. Instead, women struggle with the feelings of insignificance, martyrdom, isolation, and worst of all, a feeling of spiritual disconnection.

To add to these feelings of worthlessness, many homemakers are just not good at what they do. They cannot seem to keep ahead of the clutter. The bills do not get paid on time. They are embarrassingly late for their children's events. The laundry piles up and is never finished. Supper is seldom ready at a regular time, and when it is, the menu is either hot dogs or fast food. They *want* so much more but cannot find a way to even begin to accomplish it, especially on a daily basis. How can we do it all?

Prayer: The Key to Organizing Chaos combines the power of prayer with the activity of organizing the home or office. Discovering reminders of God's presence and love while working in the home, a realization unfolds of one's worth and value as a person and as a homemaker. Devotional sections are followed by practical, step-by-step advice to organize the specific room or problem area, such as finances or time-management.

Whether they are genetic "neatniks" mentored by meticulous mothers or those totally lacking the "organizational gene," women are expected to be the warden of the household. They are either applauded or criticized for everything that goes right or wrong in their home or in their family. They are the caretakers of mankind.

Walk with me through my personal journey from the days of being a busy, young mother to caressing the curls of grandchildren. Through those experiences I became this woman who discovered that the very heart of God can be felt and seen, even as we clean a toilet bowl. By putting the Word of God first, devotional thoughts second, prayer covering it all, and then detailed organizational advice, this book brings a spiritual method to conquering clutter and chaos.

Table of Contents

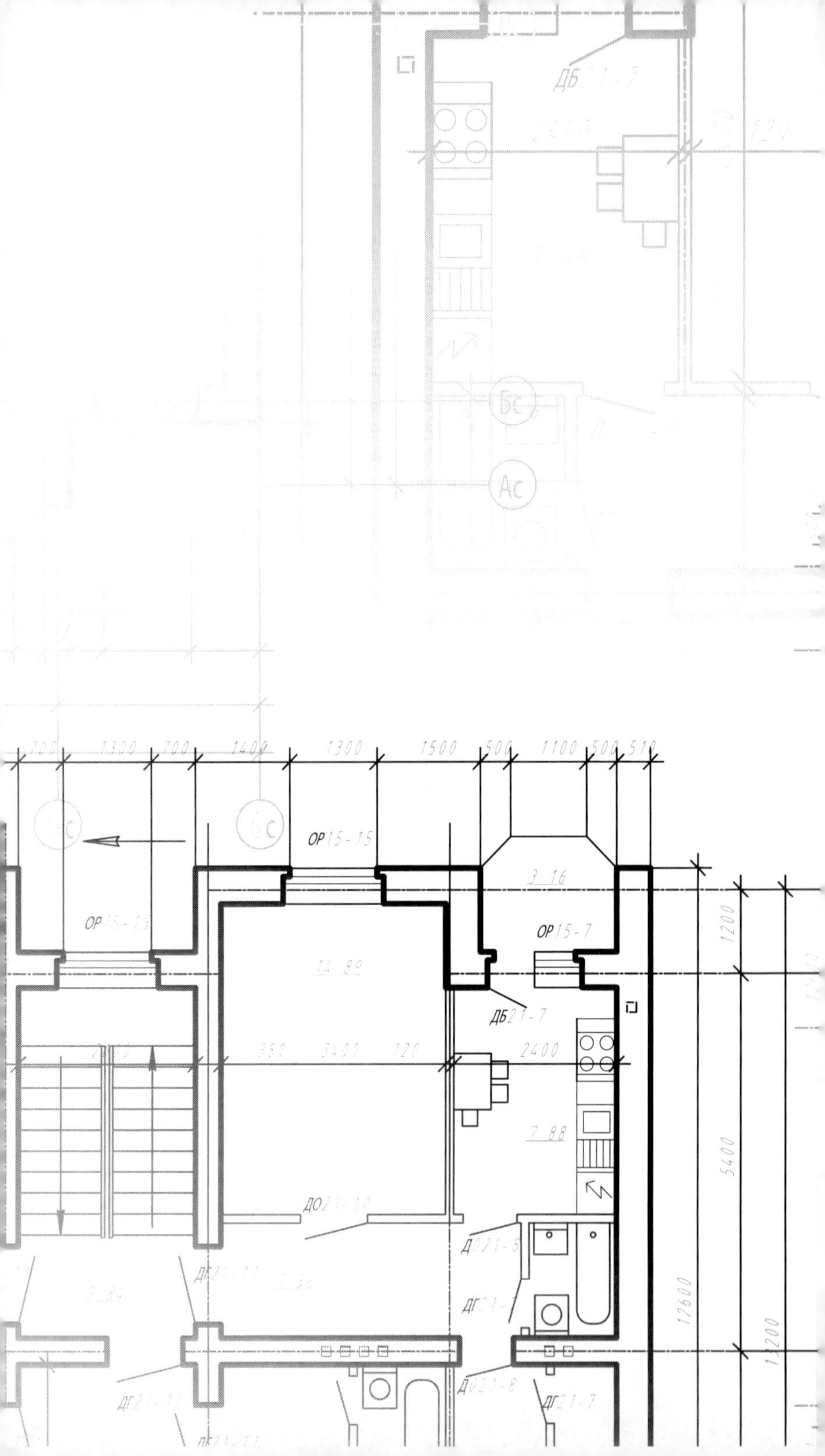

700
1300
700
1400
1300
1500
500
1100
500
510
ОР15-15
ОР15-7
ДБ21-7
2400
ДО21-10
ДО21-8
ДГ21-7
1200
5400
17600
13200

Foreword By

Treva Berends, Professional Organizer

With the birth of each of my three children I could visibly watch the amount of my laundry rapidly increase. At the time, I remember thinking that it wasn't that much of an increase. Especially since the little onesies and adorable outfits were so small. And, seeing those petite sized pieces of clothing helped me to appreciate the newborn that God had entrusted to our family.

Did you know that those small garments don't stay small? When the babies become toddlers sometimes they think it's fun to change clothes multiple times a day "just to play." And when they are potty training… well, we know about that. And, when their preferred activity is playing in the dirt pile, any dirt pile they can find, or when their favorite thing to do while playing baseball is sli-i-i-iding into base. Well, we all have our laundry woes and so when I first began to read Judy's book I quickly jumped ahead to the chapter on laundry to seek out her wisdom for this routine chore we all face.

Judy's approach is humorous as she shares practical steps and advice for those of us who are in charge of managing our homes and families. Different from other books you might read about organizing, *Prayer: The Key to Organizing Chaos* is especially refreshing to read. Judy reminds us to consider our everyday household and business tasks in relation to our Christianity and to the practicing of our faith.

Having known Judy for over twenty-five years, it is encouraging to know as I read the spiritual truths and the useful steps toward organization, that "she's been there" and she speaks from experience and from the heart.

If this is a daily devotional, can I only read one portion per day? It's too good to put down! As you read and are inspired, may I reaffirm to you what Judy and I always recommend to our clients? Be sure to schedule on the calendar specific times in your week to tackle the bite-sized areas where you need to gain order.

The journaling element in this book can also be key to your progress. Identifying and approaching the specific concerns in your space will aid you in taking action. And, as Judy so wisely advises, take the time to pray over your tasks, and offer God praise when you see and feel the results of organization!

—Treva Berends
Owner, The Organizing Specialists
theorganizingspecialists.com

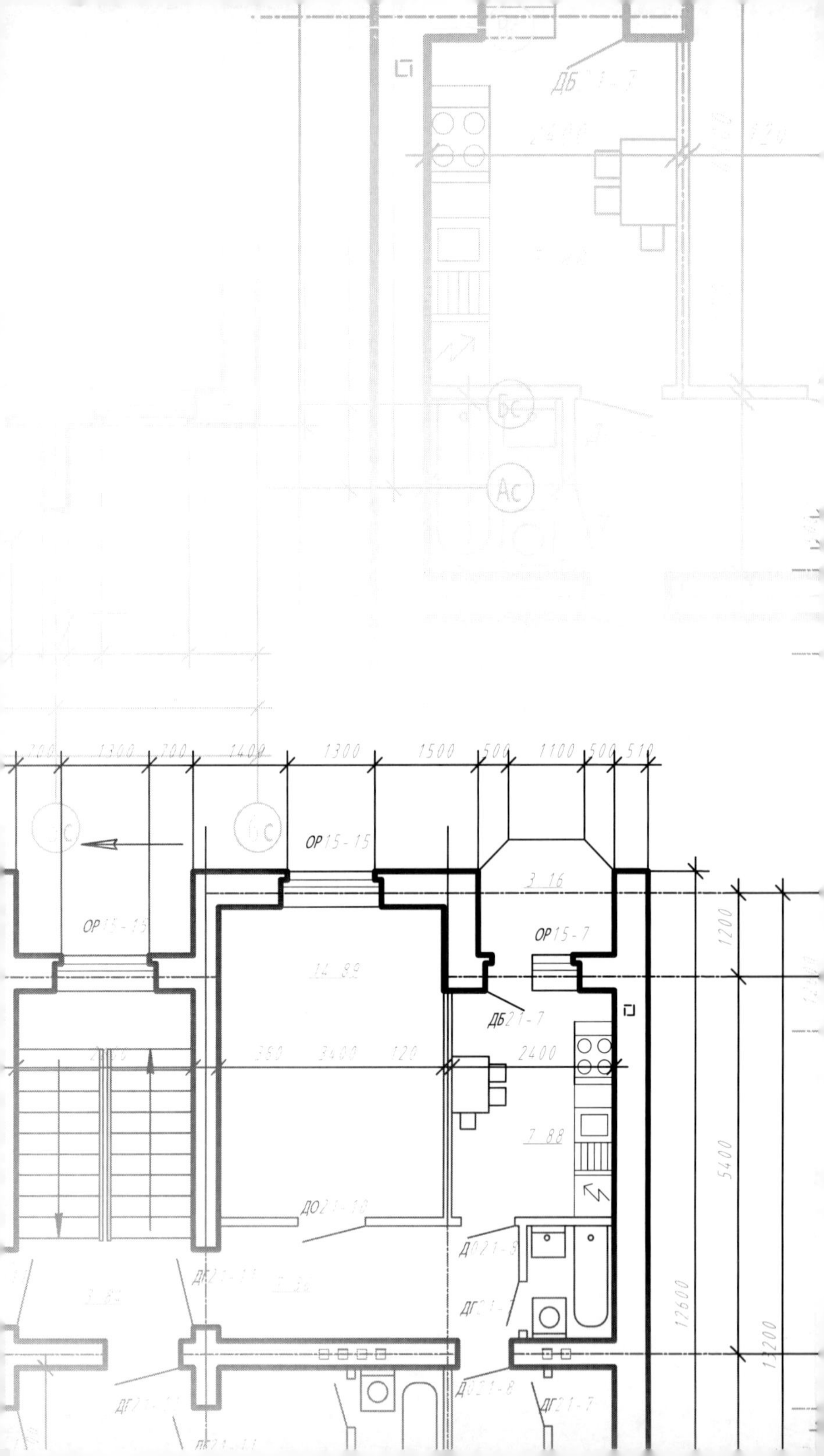
1300
1500
500
1100
500
510
ОР15-15
3.16
ОР15-7
1200
14.89
ДБ21-7
2400
7.88
5400
12600
13200

How Green is My Refrigerator . . . And I Don't Mean Money

The Kitchen

Jesus served a lot of people a lot of food and never had a dishwasher. Should we just discard all our handy appliances and not use them? Those tools can aid us in running an efficient home, entertaining friends and family and lightening our workload. Certainly He wants us to use and appreciate them. He wants the work of our hands to be pleasant as well as pleasing to Him. However, He does understand that it is hard to see beyond the workload when we are crying over a chopped onion, the laundry is not done, and we are late for an appointment. By seeing God in each part of our kitchen, we can see how important it is to Him that we have an orderly kitchen and that we use the food wisely that He has given us.

We probably spend more time in the kitchen than in any other room of the house. How can we use our kitchens for the Lord? By praying over this kitchen and all that it holds, we can seek a new guidance to organize, store, and care for each utensil and appliance.

O Lord, You created every morsel of food that has ever been grown on this earth. You created the sun to warm it, the rain to water it, and the earth to grow it. I have no doubt that You can help me bring order to the area where I will prepare food for my family. Help me to divide the clutter away from the food areas, and help me to find a plan that will enable my entire family to enjoy mealtimes in a clean, orderly kitchen. Be present while I work. Thank You, Lord Jesus, for every dish, every pan, every piece of food that You have provided for us. Help me to be a good steward with Your gifts. Amen.

Who Needs a Foot Spa—I Have a Dishwasher!

The Dishwasher

Rejoice always . . . In everything give thanks; for this is God's will for you in Christ Jesus.

—I Thessalonians 5:16, 18

Well, the dishwasher just sprang a leak! Yep, hot, soapy water is running through my kitchen carpet faster than I can run for bath towels. I felt like I just had a private "foot spa treatment" getting from the sink to the stove. How exasperating! Just when my husband is sound asleep on the couch for the first few minutes of rest after a much-too-busy week, I will be waking him soon to perform a messy, squishy task. This is far from the perfect way to spend a quiet Sunday afternoon.

Why did we have to study those verses in church today? Why not something else?

Give thanks? Rejoice? I *must* do it; I *must* see the thankful part of this. Yes, I am thankful for my husband who, although he loathes doing plumbing, is very handy with a wrench. I am thankful for an adequate supply of bath towels to soak all this water off my now only clean spot of kitchen carpet. I am thankful I have a luxury like a dishwasher and again for the loving husband who insisted on buying it when our children were all so young.

Now to rejoice! I rejoice in His Spirit that gives me quick peace and patience in such a trying situation. I am sure the Lord sees my broken dishwasher loaded with dirty dishes, my wet carpet, wet towels, wet knees, and wet socks and has compassion for me because He loves me.

That running, gushing, hot water reminds me of the torrent of warm love He pours out to me each moment if I will just lay down my life like a kitchen carpet and soak up His love for me!

Have you seen God in your dishwasher today?

I rejoice, Lord, and thank You for my broken, beautiful dishwasher. I want to see You in everything, and Your Spirit has spoken to my heart today with broken plumbing and hot water. How I love You and desire to let Your love pour over me. Use me to pour Your love into the lives of others today. I am praying in the name of Jesus. Amen.

Laser Beams and Fingernails

Cleaning the Stove

For even as the body is one and yet has many members, and all the members of the body, though they are many, are one body, so also is Christ. For by one Spirit we were all baptized into one body, whether Jews or Greeks, whether slaves or free, and we were all made to drink of one Spirit. For the body is not one member, but many.

—I Corinthians 12:12–14

Pushed out of the running for first place by a porcelain fixture, cleaning the stove-top and oven rank second on the list of my three most dreaded household chores. Every stove manufacturer seems to strive for the "Most Grooves to Clean" or "Most Hidden Wires" or "Most Screws in the Oven Door" awards. If there were such awards, my stove would take the gold, the silver, and the bronze in all divisions! What was I thinking? Why didn't I select one of those smooth, ceramic-topped, self-cleaning oven brands? I seem to have an attachment to the broken, peeling, and brown fingernails acquired from doing such jobs as this one.

I start with the racks in the oven. I love cleaning gooey pie dribbles from each section of wire. Next I'll conquer the top and sides of the oven. Don't bump the light bulb, don't spray the thermostat, but get all the baked chicken grease off them. Then, move on to the bottom of the oven. A spatula is needed to retrieve and remove the fused remains of good intentions: one chocolate chip cookie cinder, three pools of scalloped potato drips, and a large circle where the apple crisp overflowed and caught on fire. Dousing it with salt seemed like such a good idea at the time! Finally, I'll clean the oven door. Every little screw is deeply set so only a laser beam or a woman's fingernail, whichever I seem to have handy, can get inside to clean it. You know which one I will have to use.

Close the oven and attack the top of the stove. My gas stove is especially challenging. Remove each burner, burner plate, and the entire stove top, and wash it all. Clean the inside, but be careful. There are no less than 89 wires running in all directions to control lights, thermostats, and timers. Narrowly escaping electrocution, it is now time to clean the broiler unit. I have mastered several new yoga positions in order to reach all the way back into mine. Ah, finished at last. Put it all back together, and close the door. A clean stove! Just in time to start cooking dinner.

This stove has more parts than a box of Tinker Toys, yet it only does one thing. It cooks! Think of your church as one large stove. Some are racks, supporters. Some are wires, carrying a load of "electrical" messages. Some are broilers, ready for the hottest jobs. Some are handles; they direct. Some are thermostats, silent but controlling the whole operation by constant prayer. Yet all these members compose the one body, the body of believers. All are necessary, all are important. Without one member's contribution, the whole stove or church cannot function properly. Now tear your stove apart and start cleaning. Begin thanking God that it is made of several parts, yet it does one major job. As that stove prepares your food, so the body of believers work together to prepare food for a hungry world. That food is the Good News of Jesus Christ.

O dear God, please reveal to me my job in Your great plan. I want to serve You, I want to be a working part of the body of Christ and let others know about You. Please show me where my place in this plan is and what part I have. Help me to begin feeding hungry friends today. Thank You for allowing me to do this. Amen.

"Even if you're on the right track,
you'll get run over if you just sit there."
Will Rogers

Stuck on Stickies

Refrigerator

I know your deeds, that you are neither cold nor hot; I would that you were cold or hot. So because you are lukewarm, and neither hot nor cold, I will spit you out of My mouth.

—Revelation 3:15–16

Ranking third on my list of those three most thankless household jobs is cleaning the refrigerator. Why? Let me start by complaining. You can work on the refrigerator for hours, close the door, and you can't see a thing you have done! Who likes to hide all that cleanliness?

Start at the freezer section. If you're in a hurry and don't wait for it to defrost or warm up, your dishcloth starts sticking, leaving little fuzzy "stickies" here, there, and everywhere. So, you wait a little longer and start cleaning off all the little spots of gummy ice cream, fruit syrups, spilled popsicles, dehydrated vegetable bits, and lest you forgot, your "stickies." By now, your dishwater is cold from plunging a half-frozen dishcloth into it so many times, so you make new, hot, sudsy clean water.

Ah! Now tackle the refrigerator section. You remove all the little bowls containing a tablespoon of moldy this and a dab of sour that. Look, the dishwasher is full of dirty bowls and jars! No matter, you plod on removing each shelf, washing and drying them to a sparkle. Don't forget your fruit and vegetable bins. Who would have thought a carrot could get so wrinkled? You study it for craft possibilities. Perhaps if you matched it with that shriveled sweet potato ... all right, toss it. Upon removing the bins, you find some hardened pools of unidentified former liquids the consistency of peanut brittle. After soaking the pools with hot water and scraping with a razor blade for an hour or so, you are finally ready to wash the crisper drawers, returning the few remaining edible vegetables.

Now you clean the motor. Look at that hot old motor with all its dust . . . and it is so easy to reach. The old stand-on-your-head routine while running a vacuum hose always works. Snap back on the pretty motor cover panel, close the doors and there you see . . . nothing. Everything is hidden from view, and now you can proceed to clean up the mess you have made of your kitchen!

Our Christian lives can be likened to a refrigerator ready to clean. He says He knows our works, and we are lukewarm! Yes, we are often like that cold freezer that is finally warm enough to clean or like that hot motor that is cooled down enough to be vacuumed. God would have us be exactly like that refrigerator, either too hot or too cold, rather than the way we are. God forbid that we are frigid and frozen toward His love and grace. But, are we "hot" enough? Are we fired up every moment of every day? Our lukewarm state repulses God and it should repulse us, too, if we are taking an honest look at ourselves. Let's get our motors burning with the fuel of the Word and heat up our souls and the souls around us.

O dear God, fill me with enthusiasm that can come only from Your Spirit. God, I want to be on fire for You. Forgive any lazy, cold thoughts that I have had. Warm me with Your Word; fill me with Your Spirit anew that I may touch lives today. Amen.

A Crumby Affair

The Toaster

Thou wilt keep him in perfect peace whose mind is stayed on thee because he trusteth in thee.

—Isaiah 26:3, KJV

If there is one food in life I love, it is toast. Why? Toast is crispy on the outside yet warm and soft on the inside. That warmth melts peanut butter and jelly into a glossy duo serving as nutrition and dessert all rolled into one. Toast with peanut butter can be my breakfast, toast with peanut butter and jelly can be my lunch, and toast with peanut butter and honey can be my dessert after dinner. Not only do I love toast, I have raised a whole following of toast lovers.

Being a connoisseur of toast, I find you must have a good toaster to get just the right taste. My original toaster was a wedding gift. After having endured several butter knives down its sides to retrieve crusts (for I love toasted crusts the best) it began to have problems. When you pushed the button down, it stayed down. Oh, it toasted just fine, but it would not pop up unless you forcefully pushed the handle upward. Next, it lost its handle completely from being hit so often. We became used to this and would just stay nearby and gingerly nudge the tip of the tiny remaining piece of handle.

When Mother came to visit, she elected to fix her own breakfast after getting everyone else off to school. I went to start the laundry. After a few minutes I heard some yelling in the kitchen and smelled burned toast. I ran to her aid only to find her pulling the plug and shouting something about me not telling her it didn't pop up, and where was the handle, anyway? Moments later she was picking out the charred remains of her bread, offering to clean the toaster and empty the crumbs. From the bottom of the toaster came a small mountain of crumbs. Suggesting I either clean my toaster more often or make toast with a fire extinguisher handy, she told me how fortunate I was not to have had a small fire. To my chagrin, Mother appeared to be right again.

How much difference that broken handle made in the performance of that toaster! Though we have tried several ways to fix it, the lever always stayed down. Like the handle and lever on that toaster, our minds are the levers of our spirit and body. Whatever thought our mind "stays" on, our body and spirit will reflect. If our mind "stays" on the lusts of the flesh, our body seeks sinful pleasure, our spirit reveals emptiness. Charred toast and wrong living both leave bitter tastes and are useless. But if our mind "stays" on God, on his Word, our body and spirit reflect peace, His peace. As heat can toast bread, God's presence can warm our spiritual being. Pop a piece of your mind into God's "toaster" and stay a while.

Our dear Heavenly Father, please help my mind stay and concentrate on You today. Help me to remember Your words that I have read; help me to meditate on these as I go about my work today. Use Your Word to keep me from sinning today and to warm my heart with the joy of knowing You. Because of Jesus, I pray. Amen.

Chop, Drop, and Bleed

The Butcher Knife

For the word of God is living and active and sharper than any two-edged sword, and piercing as far as the division of soul and spirit, of both joints and marrow, and able to judge the thoughts and intentions of the heart.

—Hebrews 4:12

Chop! Chop! Chop! That is what I would like to be able to do. There are those people who can handle sharp knives, and there are those of us who should not even be allowed to be near one. Thankfully, I was not born to a band of gypsies who made their living throwing knives at balloons and people.

While owning and operating a restaurant, my mother-in-law gave me a heavy-handled butcher knife. She knew I did a lot of cooking, so this would be so helpful to me, right? Wrong. It seems that I chop more than vegetables every time I use it. I have gotten to the point of keeping my hand in my pocket if I have a bandage on it because I know my husband will say, "Been chopping celery again, I see." Painful, but true.

Even paring knives are too much for me. I show more fine cuts on my fingers than my chopping block has. Because of my utter lack of dexterity in the knife department, my husband refuses to sharpen my butcher knife beyond semi-dull, and the paring knives work best on butter.

Consider for a moment the comparison given to us in our verse between the Word of God and a sharp sword. It is "... living and active and sharper than any two-edged sword ... ." If it were left to be like my own butcher knife, it would have to be dull, used by a careless person. But instead, God left His Word for us sharp, piercing, and powerful no matter who is wielding His "sword." The sword will do its own work. And He need not add to it or update it or keep constantly sharpening it. It is sharp enough for all time. It can divide our soul, our spirit, our body and discern the very thoughts, intentions, and attitudes of our hearts.

I pray God's "butcher knife" is used every day in our kitchens and homes. May we just keep our fingers or lives out of its way and let it work in us.

Thank you, Lord, for Your "butcher knife." Keep me in Your Word; review these verses in my mind all day long as I work. God, touch hearts in people who have heard Your Word, causing them to understand it and seek You. Help me to be an instrument for You today. Amen.

Specks and Blobs

Rubber Spatula

Knowing that the testing of your faith produces endurance. And let endurance have its perfect result, that you may be perfect and complete, lacking nothing.

—James 1:3–4

For weeks, my rubber spatula has been broken. How I have missed it. I have resented leaving those little dabs of food stuck to the bowl because my spoon cannot get them all. Finally, I have purchased a new one. But this new one is even better and more appreciated than the old one. Not just because I need it so badly, but also because I bought it on sale! There's nothing like a bargain to boost one's spirits while shopping.

I could hardly wait to bake a cake and scrape that bowl absolutely clean with my new spatula. Having scraped that bowl, I admired its smooth, clean inside. Should I even wash that bowl or just place it back in the cupboard? It could fool the sharpest eye.

How much our lives are like the dirty bowl when God has to use a "rubber scraper" of circumstances on us to remove all our filth and evil habits that want to cling to our souls. Oh, He could be easier on us by using a spoon, but small bits of sin would be left clinging to us. How pleased He must be when we are joyful over His "rubber spatula" scraping away at us so He may present us "... faultless before the presence of His glory with exceeding joy" (Jude 24). Isn't God's grace and forgiveness even *better* than a rubber spatula? He chooses to forget our sins and there isn't anything left. There's no more pleasing sight than a clean bowl.

Turn on those beaters, mix in that bowl and evaluate what He needs to scrape out of your life.

Dear Father, You see the need in my life for Your scraper. Please forgive my disobedient heart and help me to rid my life of those habits that are clinging to it. Dear God, I want to be clean. Thank You for loving me so much that You want to have me become faultless like Your Son. In His name I pray. Amen.

Spiderman Stemware

Everyday Dishes or Fine China

May the Lord reward your work, and your wages be full from the Lord, the God of Israel, under whose wings you have come to seek refuge.

—Ruth 2:12

Thus says the Lord, "Restrain your voice from weeping, and your eyes from tears, for your work shall be rewarded," declares the Lord, "and they shall return from the land of the enemy."

—Jeremiah 31:16

Behold, I am coming quickly, and My reward is with Me to render to every man according to what he has done.

—Revelation 22:12

If you were to come to supper on an average night, you would see the table set with my everyday dishes. Now, by "everyday," I mean these are the dishes that are unmatched, but useable and practical. Though I am now blessed with a new set of "freezer to oven" dishes, I still cling to some old standbys at every meal. My old brown, melamine platter with two large chips is just the right size for our family. And, who could refuse using the cut glass butter dish that was my son's Christmas present years ago. Tupperware salt and pepper shakers, a white melamine sugar bowl, a milk glass toothpick holder, a striped glass, a Superhero glass, one white Pyrex and one clear glass coffee mug, and pieces from two sets of silverware complete the table setting. It would give Martha Stewart hives just looking at it!

But when company is coming, the picture is completely different. I use my best china, serving dishes to match the china, matching water glasses, a table cloth, candles or flowers at the center, and real cloth napkins. Not elegant, but my best.

And did you ever notice that we store these two types of dishes so differently? We keep one set stacked in the most convenient kitchen shelf for daily use. However, we display our china in a fine cabinet where the linens and silver are also kept spotless.

Will Christians be sorted in heaven like everyday dishes and fine china? Some were serviceable but did not present themselves spotless or without chips. But some may be displayed or more richly rewarded because they desired to work as a matched set, complementing other Christians' work. Because they spent their days reflecting Christ's pattern for their lives, they did not allow themselves to be chipped or stained by the world.

The Word clearly states our *works* will be tried and our reward in heaven will be according to the worth of our works here on earth. Do you wish to be only an everyday dish? Oh, that we would all desire to be fine china, highly regarded by God, highly displayed, and richly rewarded.

O dear God, today I wish to set the table of the world around me with the best that You can present in me. I give You myself today to be used to compliment other Christians' work, to reflect You as so desirable that many will want to sit at Your table. I pray in the precious name of Jesus. Amen.

Push, Burp, and Store
Seals

In Him, you also, after listening to the message of truth, the gospel of your salvation–having also believed, you were sealed in Him with the Holy Spirit of promise.

—Ephesians 1:13

Seals are not something we think of at all; in fact, we take them for granted. Seals are round about us all day, yet we hardly notice them. Do you realize your freezer and refrigerator depend on the seal around their doors to hold that cold air inside and the hot air outside? Or look at the seal on your oven door that keeps that hot air inside and the cooler air outside. Yet every time we open their doors, we "break" their seal. Consider plastic bowls and "re-sealable" plastic bags that lock in the fresh flavors of our foods. And you seal an envelope when you lick it, pasting the flap shut.

Yes, we hardly notice the existence of seals. In Ephesians 1:13, it states *we* are sealed by the Holy Spirit. Are we like refrigerator doors, oven doors, envelopes, or plastic bowls? Can our seal by the Holy Spirit be broken and then put back time and time again? When we accept Christ's purchase of our life by his gift of salvation, *we are sealed once and for all.* That seal remains intact until we are delivered to our heavenly home, never to be disturbed by anyone or anything.

How precious the seals around my home have become since I realized how precious my own seal is. Have you found some seals in your home? Are you sealed? If not, accept Christ's gift today. If so, each time you open a sealed something or other, rejoice in the promise that the Holy Spirit has sealed you unto Christ Himself.

O dear God, I feel Your assurance when I realize that your Spirit has sealed me into Your family, and no one can remove me. Help me today to feel this assurance each time I touch any seals in my home. I am praying in Jesus' name. Amen.

As a rule, a man's a fool
For when it's hot, he wants it cool.
When it's cool, he wants it hot,
Never liking what he's got.
As quoted from our dear, adopted grandmother,
Laverne Kinne

Laverne had a happy outlook on every aspect of life and certainly learned the art of contentment in her eighty-plus years God gave her on this earth. As our dearest neighbor, our children "adopted" her because their real grandparents lived so far away. In turn, she "adopted" them since she was never blessed with any children of her own. She will always remain dear in our hearts.

Chocolate Chip Smelling Salts

Cookie Jars

Not that I speak from want; for I have learned to be content in whatever circumstances I am. I know how to get along with humble means, and I also know how to live in prosperity; in any and every circumstance I have learned the secret of being filled and going hungry, both of having abundance and suffering need.

—Philippians 4:11–12

Can there be a happy home without a cookie jar? Not at my house! The cookie jar can be the cornerstone of building a good marriage if it is filled with good cookies. Have you ever seen a husband get angry at his wife when he reaches into the cookie jar? Certainly not!

The first word our children learned was not "Mama" or "Dada" but "coo-o-o-o-kie." At the same time they were learning to walk, they learned to climb on a chair, go up the cupboard front, crawl across the counter, and dig into the cookie jar. Of course, they learned all this from their father.

A full cookie jar has saved many a day at our house. After a hard day at school where they only feed children instant potatoes and stringy baked chicken (so my kids said!), a full cookie jar hit the spot. When my husband comes home from work reporting that not one thing went right all day, I wave the cookie jar under his nose, pour him a glass of milk, and settle him into his favorite chair.

Of course, when the cookie jar is empty it is a completely different story. Isn't there anything good to eat in the house? What have I done all day? Couldn't I have at least bought some cookies and tried to fake it? At this point, the only one who doesn't turn on me is the dog.

And that is only because I give him the crumbs when the jar is empty.

Our spiritual state should be like that cookie jar. We should know how to be "full" both spiritually and physically, thanking and praising God for it. We should know how to be "empty" or suffering needs, but still praise and thank God for seeing us through it. The writer of these verses, Paul, knew what it was to be wealthy, to be poor, to be hungry, to be full, to have, and to lack. But Paul knew contentment in bad times as well as good times. He looked for God's peace and love at all times. He was perceptive about what God was doing in his life. Paul knew what it was to be a cookie jar.

Is your cookie jar full or empty today? If it is empty, begin thinking of reasons to praise the Lord in spite of circumstances. If it is full, thank Him for the "cookies" He has given you. Be more than a good cookie, be a good cookie jar!

O dear Heavenly Father, You know where I am at today. You see the need in my life to learn contentment. I want to look at my situation through Your eyes and have an attitude of thankfulness for it. Please help me to do that today. Thank You. Amen.

Tub-ee or Not Tub-ee
Canisters

In those days Hezekiah became mortally ill. And Isaiah the prophet the son of Amoz came to him and said to him, "Thus says the Lord, 'Set your house in order, for you shall die and not live.'"

—II Kings 20:1

For this reason I left you in Crete, that you might set in order what remains, and appoint elders in every city as I directed you.

—Titus 1:5

For God is not a God of confusion but of peace, as in all the churches of the saints. But let all things be done properly and in an orderly manner.

—I Corinthians 14:33

Do you remember your first canister set? Mine was a gift of love. Six of my nieces and nephews pooled their money, buying me a set of tin canisters for a wedding gift. Nested together in four different sizes with tightly fitted lids, they were decorated with pretty flowers. For many years, this row of canisters stored my flour, sugar, coffee, and tea.

The day of replacement came at a garage sale. Picture a brand new set of ceramic canisters for five dollars. I couldn't resist! My countertop became transformed with this new look, yet I could not just discard the old set. I transferred the food, and continued to use them for dried fruits and other sugars. What more could a housewife ask for than two sets of canisters?

Throughout our homes, canisters and storage containers of various sizes help organize objects we use everyday. If you go into any discount store, storage containers have become big business. We can keep anything from cotton balls and puzzle parts to blankets and basketballs by storing them in some type of container.

An organized home is pleasant to live in. An organized home is even pleasing to God. Organization in our lives in all areas pleases God. In these Bible verses, we learn God wanted lives and estates put in order, church leadership put in order, and our spiritual gifts used in an orderly fashion.

Order is a necessity to the smooth operation of any business, church, or home. Christians should feel no less responsibility for running an orderly, well-organized church than they feel for their jobs. Likewise, every Christian homemaker should understand that God is pleased with orderliness in the home. This does not mean sterile or perfect living conditions; just orderly. Orderliness leads to less confusion, more tranquility, and even to cleanliness. Orderliness shows you have taken the responsibility of running a home that is not only pleasant for your family but also pleasing to God.

Dust off those canisters, and line them up. Get out your empty storage bins and arrange them by sizes. Does the rest of your house match this order? Does your life match this order? Setting your house and life in order makes a more pleasant home for you and your family, as well as being pleasing to the Lord.

Dear Father, I feel that my home and my thoughts are in disarray many days. Help me to focus on putting things in order. Help me to start corner by corner, room by room and create an orderly, pleasant, neat setting for my family. I want to please You in this way because You have given me Your Son, Jesus. Amen.

Frosted with Sprinkles, Please

Cookie Cutters

Then God said, "Let Us make man in Our image, according to Our likeness; and let them rule over the fish of the sea and over the birds of the sky and over the cattle and over all the earth, and over every creeping thing that creeps on the earth." And God created man in His own image, in the image of God He created him, male and female He created them.

—Genesis 1:26–27

And He is the image of the invisible God, the first-born of all creation.

—Colossians 1:15

What fun to roll and cut out our favorite cookies fashioned with our favorite cookie cutters. I am personally into bizarre cookie cutters. Mine include lips, a foot, a tooth, and a Michigan map—both peninsulas. It has been fun to share these with the children and watch them bite off toes and cities! Every season or holiday has its own special cookie design. How pretty the plate is, filled with cookies shaped like pumpkins or Christmas trees or Easter bunnies or animal characters.

Beyond the idea of cookies, I have said some children are "cookie cutters" of their parents. Don't some children look like shrunken versions of their parents? More than just the same looks, they seem to even have the same mannerisms as the parent. Are we all just cut from the same mold?

Have you ever thought of *yourself* as being cut out with a cookie cutter? Yes, God created us in His own image. Yet, each person is totally different and unique in his or her own way. But when we receive Christ as our

Savior, God's eyes behold us as if we were all cut from the same pattern. He sees each of us as though He were seeing Christ Himself, faultless and perfect and characterized only by His loving Son.

Plus, we are a "no-bake" recipe! We will never be browned nor baked in the oven of hell because we are perfect "cookies" just the way He cuts us out.

Do you want to be a "no-bake" cookie cut from the Master's cookie cutter? Ask Christ to be your Savior today, forgiving all your sins. Or, if you are already one of God's perfect "no-bake cookies" why not start decorating the table of the world and let them know the pattern you enjoy wearing each day. No matter how you slice it, there's no better cookie pattern to be!

Thank You, dear Heavenly Father, for the reminder that I am made in Your image. Dear God, may I show You to everyone around me today by being as pleasing as the fragrance of a cookie being baked. Thank You for allowing me to decorate this world for You. Amen.

Cling-Ons

Refrigerator Magnets

Therefore, since we have so great a cloud of witnesses surrounding us, let us lay aside every encumbrance, and the sin which so easily entangles us, and let us run with endurance the race that is set before us. Fixing our eyes on Jesus, the author and perfecter of faith …

—Hebrews 12:1–2a

Growing up in a family of five children, the front of our refrigerator was only ever covered with sticky fingerprints. The invention of refrigerator magnets has changed all that. Today we have a combination of memo board, family pictorial history, day-planner, and school menu/events file all on the front of the refrigerator.

Then, each magnet that holds an item, carries a message in itself. Many are souvenirs, reminding us of places we or friends have visited. There are cutesy ones that remind us not to eat, what to eat, what not to say, who to love (rainforests, Mom, and grandparents always head the list), what to hate (environmental pollution, and toxic waste), when to rise in the morning (early bird?), and how late to party at night. There must be millions of magnet shapes and ideas. But each has the same use and purpose. Put it near anything metal and it attaches itself to it. Put a paper or photo under it and it is held in place.

Just like a refrigerator magnet holds down a message on your refrigerator, sin becomes a weight, a magnet, holding us back from fully living our lives for Christ. Magnets use their "force" to pin down or attach themselves to the metallic surfaces. Sin uses its "force" to pin us down or attach us to a lifestyle that displeases Christ and slows us down in any effort toward spiritual growth.

As you complete this section of this devotional, I challenge you to cast off, set aside every "encumbrance," every magnet holding you back from concentrating on Jesus' plan for your life. With the decision to free yourself from sin's "magnetic force," you will be able to move forward, possibly even run toward new goals, new growth.

How will you finish your "race?" Will you have weights on your shoulders? Will your "magnets" keep you pinned to the starting line? Or will you have made a decision to let Christ free you from the weight of acts or thoughts that displease God? Will you finish your race looking toward that final goal, the face of Christ?

Aren't you glad refrigerator magnets were invented? Will you ever see another one that doesn't remind you of Christ's power over sin?

Dear Father, forgive me for letting sin hold me back from living for You each moment of each day. I realize I am in a huge race—a race against time, a race against sin. I want to see Your face. I choose to fix my eyes on You because You are the origin of my being, and You will be the finisher of my life and future. I accept the challenge to not only run my race well, but to daily walk with You. I am praying in the precious name of Jesus. Amen.

My Kitchen Journal

"I promise to work on this room and not take on the organization of any other room until this orderly kitchen begs for me to cook in it!"

1. Circle or name the three major problem areas in your kitchen, prioritizing them with numbers.

   - Countertop clutter
   - Tabletop clutter
   - Spices/baking area/cookbooks/baking pans
   - Not enough drawer space
   - Plastic storage bowls/bowl sets/casserole dishes
   - Good "china" or extra dishes storage
   - Under-sink area
   - Pantry/food storage
   - Other:

____

____

2. Because I know God created all the food we eat, my prayer for God's customized solution is the following:

____

____

____

3. The Scripture that has encouraged me to organize this kitchen is the following:

____

____

____

4. In order to complete my prioritized tasks, the supplies that I will need are the following:

    - Three containers for Trash, Donate, Save
    -
    -
    -
    -

(This would be a good time to read and follow along with "It's Time to Organize That Kitchen.")

5. (*To be completed after your kitchen organizing job is finished.*)
   I see that God helped me organize my kitchen. My feelings about this room are now (include today's date):

___

___

___

___

6. My *one year later* journal entry about this room is (include the date):

___

___

___

It's Time to Organize That

Kitchen

Take a tour of your kitchen as if you were visiting it for the first time. My personal, best organizing happens when I work from *one side of the room around to the other.* I have called this "Circular Organization." If this can work for you, start on one end of the cupboards.

Get ready to work. Here is how we will conquer clutter *and* chaos:

Get three containers ready: Trash, Donate, and Save.

Countertop Clutter

Your first step will be to completely empty your countertops. Sort and eliminate all *small appliances* from the counter that you do not use at least three or more days a week. *Limit* the number of small appliances or other utensils that can be returned. You want to create a feeling of openness.

Contain those papers! Begin using a small organizational *drawer unit* labeled for "School," "Phone and Address Books," or whatever you need at hand but cannot fit into a kitchen cupboard drawer. Do *not* use this new drawer unit for bills. We will create a mail/ bill paying center later. If school papers are a problem, perhaps you could try small eight-inch by ten-inch baskets for each child and one for upcoming events or papers to sign and return to school. Whatever method you choose, always be determined to *contain* papers.

Use your walls to keep items up off the counter. Cup hooks for extra mugs, hooks for keys, or a shelf for baskets or the drawer unit will leave the countertop free for what it is designed to do: prepare and serve meals. Always choose to stack or go upward, avoiding sprawl.

A PERSONAL ORGANIZING STORY

We had a pocket-emptying-to-the-counter problem at our house. With limited counter space to prepare food, this became a bit of a sore spot with me. I really did not want to nag my husband into a solution, so I decided to use my organizing-client-prayer-method instead. But how could I give him space in "my space"? The answer that God kept putting in my mind was "measure." So, I measured. After measuring, I realized I did have some space that I could spare for this! Next, I simply bought a small three drawer plastic unit. The top drawer became my husband's, the middle drawer contains the address book and scrap paper for notes and the bottom drawer became a phone book drawer. Topping it all off is the caller ID module, answering machine and portable phone. My husband loved having a handy place to put his billfold, keys, work papers, and pertinent information. The next morning, he could find everything he needed. I never have touched that top drawer nor cleaned it. It is *his.* I actually *gained* storage space by sacrificing a few inches of counter space. That was the customized answer to my prayer. Thank you, Lord!

Could this work for you? Always measure any space you intend to use before purchasing a new storage unit. So often, simple solutions make a world of difference.

Cupboards

Begin at one end of the cupboards and work your way through each one purging anything broken, donating anything you no longer use (or *never* used) and then wash out each area before returning *only useable items* to the shelves and drawers.

Don't be afraid to buy some new drawer dividers, "stair step" racks to elevate spices or medications or foods located at the back of a shelf, turn-tables for small items, and shelf liners as you clean.

Definitely purge food items that are outdated or you know you will not use. This clears the way for useable items.

Try to arrange your cupboards for convenience. This is a suggested "grouping" for each cupboard:

- Dishes and glasses above/near dishwasher
- Silverware near dishes and table
- Frequently used condiments (sugar, salt, etc.) near table and/or stove
- A cupboard for baking ingredients
- Cookbooks near baking ingredients
- Pots and pans near stove
- Baking pans near stove
- Pot holders and hot pads near stove
- Cooking utensils near stove
- Spices near stove
- Dry foods may be stored above stove (pasta, rice, etc.)
- Extra foods in pantry area

Some cleaning supplies usually end up under the sink. Consider the ages of children living or visiting the home before doing this. Remove cleaning supplies to an upper shelf as needed. Purchase an under-sink unit or baskets to make visibility and removal of any items easier.

(We will also talk about cleaning items under "Laundry" and "Cleaning Supplies" later.)

Trash Can

I prefer to keep the trash under my sink, out of view, on a pull out arm for ease in filling and emptying. If it must be in the room, purchase one with a good lid and that adds some style to your room. You spend a lot of time in that kitchen. No use looking at a beat up waste can! Put it as close to the sink as you can, but try to keep it inconspicuous.

Kitchen Table

Is your kitchen table a magnet for items the family drops when they are on the run? This is a problem that will take the cooperation of everyone to eliminate. Provide new receptacles for their papers (your new drawer unit?), a few hangers for keys, and baskets to hold cell phones, gadgets, items from pockets, items needed daily, etc. After you sort through the items on the table, have everyone put their items away, then polish the table and *commit to eating meals at that table, together.*

General Kitchen "Clutter"

Everyone wants his or her items of necessity to be right at hand when he or she walks out the door. The kitchen is always the place to lay them so they are "handy." Wrong. By creating new "centers" for individuals, you can begin to break some habits that have contributed to the clutter. New hangers or baskets in or near a closet help establish new habits. Everyone can grab his or her own items from a hook or basket and grab a jacket on the way out the door. This gives them a *specific area of their own.* This "creation" on your part will begin to dispel some of that morning mayhem when someone cannot find their keys, their papers to return to school, an item to give a friend, etc. The bottom line is *stress.* You will bring a calmer spirit in the kitchen each morning and, hopefully, each evening as items are put away and found again in their proper places.

Finishing the Job

Trash Bag: Just like it says, throw it out!

Donate Bag/Box: Take these items to the nearest non-profit organization ASAP and leave them. D*o not* dig through them and take anything back. Remember, the longer you keep these items before donating, the more you will be tempted to reclaim them for your kitchen.

Save Bag/Box: Sort all items according to the person they belong to, the purpose or use of the items, or the rooms in which they belong. Save all necessary papers and put in files, give individuals a stack of their own to put away, disperse and put away items from other rooms. Do this quickly or else you will have accumulated a box of old junk in your kitchen and will justify filling the new empty spaces with *new* junk.

Dining Room

Going hand-in-hand with the kitchen is the dining room if you are blessed enough to have one. Use the same rules as for the kitchen; just apply them in different areas. Take a close look at how many shelves and drawers are available for storage, and let's evaluate what to save. Using three containers, repeat the processes from the kitchen: Trash, Donate, Save.

China Cabinet

As you are sorting, ask yourself, "Do I really use this item?" China cabinets get used as storage bins unless you carefully scrutinize each item and determine to store only what you *actually* use. Consider if items are only used seasonally. Are some items only used for holidays or in the summer, perhaps on your deck? Then they should be stored with seasonal or holiday decorations, out of the main living area. New space found! Continue this process until the china cabinet is empty and then replace only what you use regularly and want to display.

Dining Room Table

The same rule applies as the kitchen table.

General Dining Room Clutter

Because this room is not used as often, the temptation to store items to keep "handy" is even greater. Use those same three containers. When you have sorted the clutter into individuals' piles, give it to them to put away. They will probably be a little hesitant at first. But when you give them direction and some new containers and shelving, perhaps they will begin to change those hard-to-break habits of using the dining room as a storage shed.

Finishing the Job

Now refer back to the kitchen area and make proper use of those three containers: Trash, Donate and Save. The dining room may contain more memorabilia than the kitchen, so be prepared to store it accordingly. Heirloom linens, grandmother's china or special glassware can be displayed in a cabinet or put away for the next generation. Do not let it consume your storage spaces or set the tone for a cluttered room. Memories and orderliness can survive in the same area. Knowing your available spaces and *limiting displays* can be your guideline.

Give Credit to the Lord

When you have worked through these two rooms, take time to praise and thank the Lord.

O Lord, You know this has been a hard task for me. My family is important to me. Meal time and less stress are important to me. Thank You for the direction You have given me and for the accomplishment of having order in my kitchen and dining room. Please help each one of us to keep up our part in putting things away in order to have this area continue to be one of happy memories around our tables. Thank You, Jesus. Amen

Now go back a few pages and complete your *Kitchen Journal.*

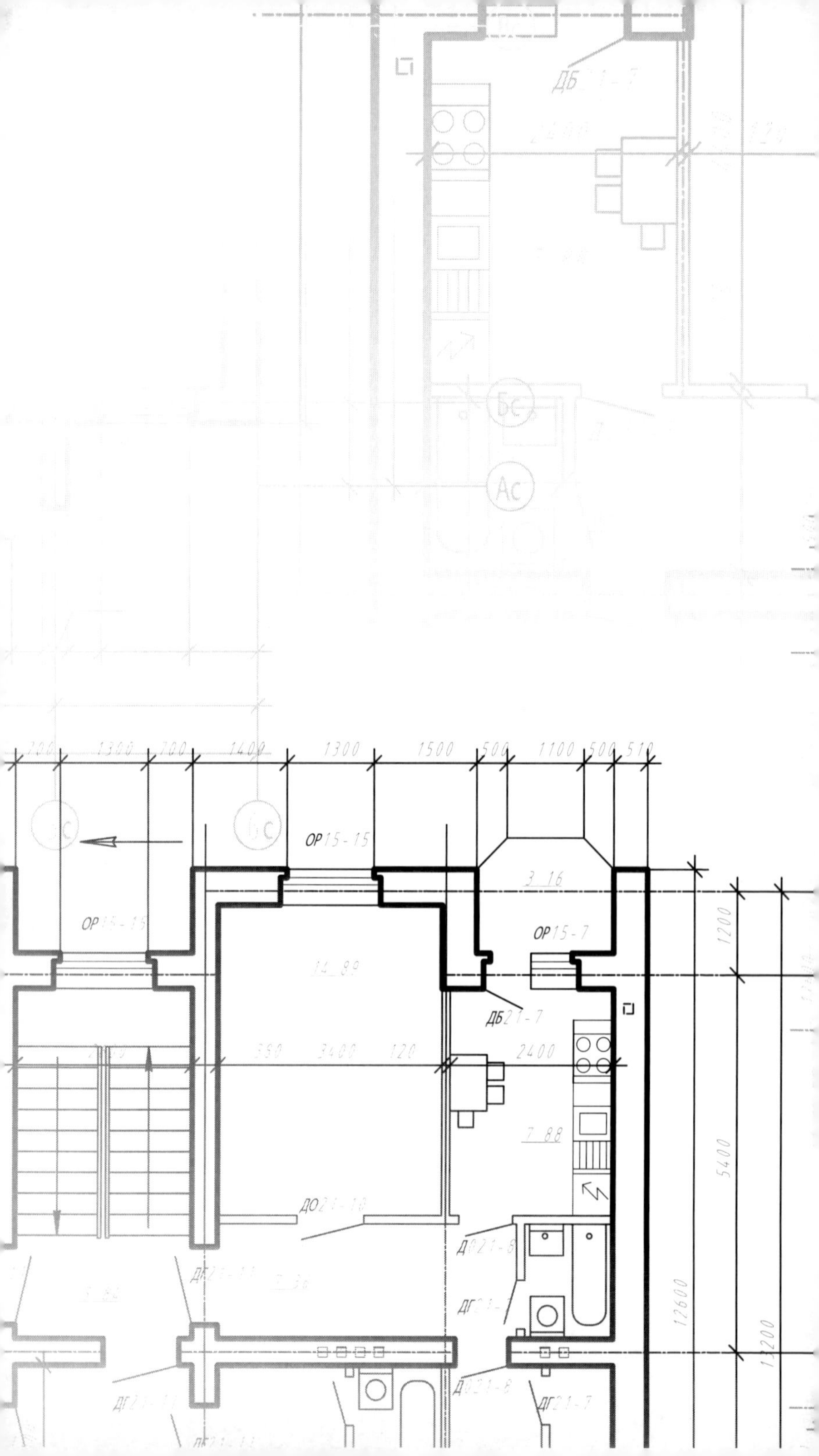

ДБ21-7
2400
Бс
Ас
700
1300
700
1400
1300
1500
500
1100
500
510
ОР15-15
3.16
ОР15-7
1200
14.89
390
3400
120
7.88
5400
ДО21-10
ДО21-8
12600
13200
ДГ21-7

The Couch Potato's Soap Opera: *As the Cushion Turns*

The Living Room/Family Room

Without exception, we feel inadequate in having guests enter our homes. We feel that our furniture is not nice enough, our home is disorganized with a lot of clutter, or we feel we cannot concentrate to have a good conversation because the guest may notice all the mess and dirt. Sound like you? God wants us to use our very biggest asset, our home, as a tool for His ministry to others. Can you get it together enough to ever do this? I am convinced that you can because He has promised to help you with whatever you need. Let's look to God's Word and be praying over this area for specific help with it.

Dear Lord, You know I want to use my living room and family room to have restful, fun evenings with my family. You know that I want to entertain my friends here but so often feel that my home is just not worthy, attractive enough, or orderly enough to have people come here and see how we really live. You know how inadequate I feel about this. Please help me with these rooms. Help me through these messages from Your Word to see the value of my home, the fact that You have provided it for me and that You want me to use it for You. Give me courage by meditating on Your Word. Give me insights into where to store things and what to throw away. Thank You for what You are going to help me do through this. Amen.

Knock, Knock, Who's There?

Doorbells

Behold, I stand at the door and knock; if anyone hears my voice and opens the door, I will come in to him, and will dine with him, and he with Me.

—Revelation 3:20

Someone called the other day and said they stopped by, rang the doorbell, but no one answered. They must have missed me. That's strange, for I had been home all day. But some of my modern conveniences cause me these inconveniences occasionally, and I am getting used to it. Who can hear the doorbell with the blow dryer running next to their ear or the vacuum droning or when in the shower? I guess I will have to get a bell that resembles the one in a firehouse that can be heard above the noise!

I should be out ringing doorbells myself, telling others of Christ's love and gift to them. But maybe they won't hear their doorbells either. Maybe I should just forget it. But in Romans 10:14, we read:

"How then shall they call upon Him in whom they have not believed? And how shall they believe in Him whom they have not heard? And how shall they hear without a preacher?"

Christ rang a lot of doorbells when He was here on earth, but few wanted to hear them ring and even fewer answered the door. John 1:11 says:

"He came unto His own and His own received him not."

No, very few wanted what He had to offer.

In Revelation 3:20, Christ is again knocking, seeking entrance. Can you believe He *never gives up?* I have not rung enough doorbells lately, but I am ringing yours now. If you have not trusted Christ as Savior, do so today. If you have already answered His "doorbell," why not do as God's Word encourages us to do: go tell others who have not heard. All it takes is one finger to push that bell. Ready? *Ring!*

O dear Heavenly Father, I have not been ringing any bells lately. Please help me to have the courage to tell others about You. Please open the heart of the one I talk to, giving them understanding of Your truth. Make me that messenger today. Thank You for this privilege You have given to me because of Jesus. Amen.

Lead Hide-a-Bed

The Sofa

Therefore, my beloved brethren, be steadfast, immovable, always abounding in the work of the Lord, knowing that your labor is not in vain in the Lord.

—I Corinthians 15:58

Probably many people own sofas similar to ours—a veritable gold mine. I make it a point to bravely pull the cushions off it at least once a year. Besides the usual collection of popcorn, paper clips, buttons and pencils, I have found dirty socks, Fisher Price toys, hair brushes, photos, and of course, loose change. I believe I could sustain a squadron of soldiers just on the junk food scraps found under those cushions.

Now, removing the cushions is the easy part of cleaning this sofa. Under its two cushions and slender little arms sits a ton of framework and a hide-a-bed. Cleaning under it requires no less than a fork-lift truck and an industrial vacuum. When it is put back in place, the room shudders and the floor sags. When I say I never move my sofa, I mean I *never* move my sofa.

How much like that sofa we should be in our determination to work for the Lord. Maybe that "work" is praying daily for missions or for loved ones who need to know about Christ, baking some cookies for a sick friend, making a phone call to a lonely elderly person, or giving your own family some extra TLC. Perhaps you can volunteer to mow the church lawn, clean the church bathrooms, help in the nursery, greet visitors, or send a card to a person who just needs to know someone cares. Maybe that work is on a foreign field or a position of great responsibility in your local church.

Whatever that "work" is that God has called you to do, be like a lead weight, unmovable. Stick at it, don't hedge, don't give up, don't even slack up. Be like my sofa, four thousand pounds of determination.

Lord, please help me to be faithful in working for You, to show others Your love through my life. Please help me to not be discouraged, to be steadfast, and not give up, ever! Amen.

"The point of having an open mind, like having an open mouth, is to close it on something solid."

G. K. Chesterton

Flappers
Doors

He who guards his mouth and his tongue, guards his soul from troubles.

—Proverbs 21:23

My family has a problem with doors. In the summer, when I get a beautiful breeze blowing through my kitchen, someone comes in and closes the door. However, in the winter when the furnace is running full blast and the wind is howling, someone comes in and leaves the door standing wide open. I am sure this is an isolated problem and my family must be one of only a few who experience the frustration of open and closed doors—at the wrong times!

And did you ever notice how much pressure is behind the door that flies open from the summer breeze or the winter gust of wind? The door simply bursts open and bangs against the nearest wall, sometimes even causing damage. Or when not latched just right, it will just pop open without warning.

How much those doors remind me of my mouth! Whenever the opportunity arises for me to say a few words of how my Lord has blessed me or testify of His love, there I sit with my mouth tightly shut. On the other hand, when someone offends me, I just flap that same mouth wide open and let out all the unkind words that should have been closed tightly inside.

Yes, our mouths are like doors. So often they are closed or open at exactly the wrong times. I pray that today we will only open or close our "doors" at the right moment.

O dear God, I offer You my mouth. Please help me to be a quiet person at the right times. Help me to bless You and to testify for You when any opportunity arises. Help me to identify these times. As I touch any doors today, remind me of my mouth, Lord. I love You. Amen.

ERMA TRIED HOUSEPLANTS, TOO

The late Erma Bombeck had a humorous view on almost every aspect of the American household. Raising houseplants was no different. Over the years, I found Erma and I had a lot in common.

> I know now that you can't take a Boston fern seriously. It'll tear your heart out. You have to know that from the moment you take it out of the nursery, it turns hostile. It doesn't want your water. It doesn't want your sun. It doesn't want your fertilizer or your Willie Nelson records. It just wants to die.
>
> So why do people buy Boston ferns in the first place? Because they need to feel challenged. You reach a stage in your life where you know you're not going to be Miss America; you're not going to win the Pillsbury Bake Off. Winning the lottery is a long shot and you've been passed over too often to have a late-night talk show of your own. So you see how long you can sustain a Boston fern.[1]

The Black Thumb

Houseplants

And I will appoint a place for My people Israel, and will plant them, that they may dwell in their own place and be moved no more, neither shall the wicked waste them anymore as formerly.

—I Chronicles 17:9

"Take this plant home, Judy. It's going to die anyway." These departing words from my mom as she handed me a sick-looking houseplant were harsh, but true. She knew that coming to my house would be a death sentence for the droopy little thing. Evidently, she didn't have the courage to just dump it out while it still had a hint of life in it. Better to send it to my home of neglect.

I have truly made an effort to be successful with my fertilizers, less water, and more sun ... or was that more water, and less sun? You see my problem. I sunburn violets, drown cactus, and over-water almost everything else. I was even entrusted with a Christmas cactus handed down from three generations. What crazy relatives would ask me to care for it? It is still living, but only because I frequently pray for it and just stay away from it.

There is a vast difference between those frail houseplants and their hardy counterparts, the outdoor plants. Many of those survive the hottest summer days, the heaviest spring rains, the coldest winter freezes. Yet raised in its correct environment, each thrives and grows.

Christians are like houseplants and outdoor plants. Some are created to grow within sheltered surroundings; some are created to go out into the harsh world and can still thrive. Yet each type is valuable to God, to their fellow Christians and to all they serve. The "houseplant"

Christian can minister, teach, and witness within his hometown or own country. The "outdoor" Christian may be led across the seas to strange lands to do those same things in a totally different environment. God is the great Planter Who places us where He wants us, just as He placed the Israelites exactly where He wanted them.

Has God called you to be a "houseplant"? Praise Him for it! Has He called you to be an "outdoor plant"? Obey His will and thank Him for it! For you see, even though we need different environments, we all thrive from the very same root system, the Lord Jesus Christ. So bloom, Christian!

O dear Heavenly Father, I want to be the "plant" You want me to be! Please give me wisdom in keeping my environment full of Your Word. Help me take time to tend Your garden, the world around me. Make me aware of opportunities You place before me. Help me to bloom, sharing Your fragrance at the right time. Thank You, Jesus, for my houseplants. Thank You for planting me, rooting me in Yourself. Amen.

My Fur-ont Door

The Front Door

Moreover, they shall take some of the blood and put it on the two door posts and on the lintel of the houses in which they eat it . . . And the blood shall be a sign for you on the houses where you live; and when I see the blood I will pass over you, and no plague will befall you to destroy you when I strike the land of Egypt.

—Exodus 12:7, 13

What is the area a visitor gazes upon to get their first impression of your home? The front door, naturally. I have visited many homes that have nice little porches or steps, a lovely door, an attractive welcome plaque or wreath, a lighted doorbell, and cushioned mat.

That *Better Homes and Garden* home was in another neighborhood when we were raising our family on our small farm. There was no magazine cover photo happening at our house. Our front door was fearlessly guarded day and night by our aging, crippled German shepherd. She left as her mark piles of fur stuck to the doormat and a body-sized brownish smudge on the siding where she leaned for support while on duty. My children never learned to hold onto a door handle, so the glass on the storm door had personalized fingerprints on both sides. The gorgeous diamond-light pattern on the inner door resembled smoked glass thanks to our wood heat. Because the same dog was allowed to lie on the rug inside the door, more of the same fur greeted you as you wiped your feet to come inside. Now mud and fur covered footprints tracked on through the house. This made a great first impression, right?

During the first Passover, God was very concerned

with the Israelites' doorways. As the angel of death moved through Egypt, that first impression meant life or death. The sight of the lambs' blood, placed there in obedience, brought life. The lack of it brought death.

As you clean and make tidy your front door, study it and remember the Israelites. Remember God's promise, "... and when I see the blood, I will pass over you ..." Are you ready to impress God with your obedience? Is your doorway or life covered with Christ's blood? How is your doorway?

Dear Jesus, thank You for reminding me today that because You shed Your blood for me, God sees me through You. You are my doorway into heaven! May I remember this each time I open my door today. Amen.

ERMA'S TAKE ON THE TV

The television was considered by Erma Bombeck as an invasion of her household and the spell it cast on her husband was nothing short of a coma for a head injury patient. Read on:

> I could have appeared in a gown made out of Astroturf and a number on my back and he would have sat with his eyes glued to the set and asked, "We out of dip?"
>
> Spectators cheer. They jump out of their chairs occasionally. They take nourishment (sometimes intravenously). Their eyes blink. But the sleeptator just sits there in front of the television set with his eyes closed. For all purposes he is somewhere between the fourth quarter and death.
>
> Enter the spouse, who truly believes her husband is asleep. She reaches over to turn off the monotone drone of the announcer when the lump speaks, "Touch that dial and you're a dead woman."[2]

Hypnovised
The Television

And when they did not agree with one another, they began leaving after Paul had spoken one parting word, "The Holy Spirit rightly spoke through Isaiah the prophet to your fathers, saying 'Go to this people and say, "You will keep on hearing but will not understand; and you will keep on seeing, but will not perceive; For the heart of this people has become dull, and with their ears they scarcely hear, and they have closed their eyes; lest they should see with their eyes, and hear with their ears, and understand with their heart and return, and I should heal them."'

—Acts 28:25–27

Some endearing terms for the word "television" have evolved in the past many years. Because we now can see its real effects, we call it such names as idiot box, boob tube, one-eyed monster, the baby-sitter, squawk box, and the centerpiece of the evening meal.

Its effect on a nine-year-old boy at cartoon time is apparent. The eyes bug out, the face is motionless, and the ears are unable to hear the word "garbage," "bedroom," or "homework." The effects on a full-grown, sports-minded man are even more devastating. The eyes are bloodshot, the mouth hangs open, and the body is paralyzed into one position for no less than three hours. The ears have heard so many whistles, buzzers, and bells that they only respond to one word: "food." The teenager seems to be the only one who can watch TV for short periods of time and then leave. They settle in for a few neat car rolls, a head-on collision, Corinthian leather, a 1950s scene of kissing in the back seat. Then to put your mind at ease, they ask for the car keys, leaving the driveway burning rubber. And we owe all of it to the television set!

Have you ever tried to vacuum when the family is watching TV? They suddenly come alive and race for the remote, setting the volume so loud the windows start vibrating. Or have you ever tried standing in front of the screen to get their attention during their favorite program? A friend of mine did that, and her family shoved her out the back door and locked it until the next meal-time.

What other machine can so absorb our minds as the television? We see it, we watch it, and we listen to it. Christ broadcast Himself to the Jewish people, but they refused to see Him as God's Holy Son even though they could really see Him physically. Christ broadcasted God's Word to them yet they refused to believe it even though they could hear Him speak. And so Christ began to be "broadcasted" abroad to the Gentiles, you and me. Many of those that saw Him and heard Him believed. Today, many believe who have not seen Him, but hear God's promise of everlasting life because Jesus Christ paid the penalty for their sins on the cross.

Are you absorbed with seeing and hearing God? Are you watching Him and hearing Him? Or is your picture screen blank or volume too low? The next time you find yourself absorbed in a television program, decide to spend as much time in God's Word and prayer as you spend with that TV. You will find it's the best channel to watch and the best "program" to hear.

Dear Jesus, I want to listen to You today and I want to see You. Please make Your Word real to me today, helping me to remember what I hear You say to me. Remind me to turn off the television and spend time with You. Thank You, Jesus. Amen.

Habits are at first cobwebs, then cables.

Spanish Proverb

Spin-Art
Cobwebs

Four things are small on the earth, but they are exceedingly wise: The ants are not a strong folk, but they prepare their food in the summer; the badgers are not mighty folk, yet they make their houses in the rocks; the locusts have no king, yet all of them go out in ranks; the lizard you may grasp with the hands, yet it is in king's palaces.

—Proverbs 30:24–28

How naïve I am! I always thought cobwebs were simply little puffs of dust that collected together here and there when the air was too dusty, like when the furnace runs. A friend said spiders make little webs and that the dust gathers on them. Incredible! I checked the dictionary, and she is right!

Therefore, I have adopted a new attitude toward cobwebs. If it took those little spiders so much work to get them up there, why should I be in such a hurry to get them down? After all, a web that long must have taken days to spin!

I have noticed that most spiders are uncannily crafty. Why is it they always seem to form cobwebs above eye level? How much easier it would be to clean if this were forbidden in a spider code-of-law. Also, they seem to go into a frenzy the night before company comes with cobwebs suddenly appearing when your guests arrive. Having a secret pact with the sun, they remain obscured until everyone is gathered around the table. In the middle of dinner, as beautiful sunshine begins beaming in the window, you spot one dangling from the chandelier directly over the meat. The children spot you eyeing it and ask what that is hanging over the table. You can picture the rest. Then too, cobwebs are not selective. I have seen them moving in the draperies of pastors' homes, on the ceilings of courtrooms, in the lights of teachers' homes, and even in the stairways of the finest churches. No, cobwebs don't care if they are in a basement or in a kitchen, just as long as you don't bother them.

Can you picture cobwebs in a king's palace? I'm sure that the royal family in England is not even aware that lowly spiders are trying to spin their little "homes" in every room of Buckingham Palace. But I'm also just as sure that those spiders are there. How wise the spider is to be able to live in a king's palace for free! How wise he is to stay high up the walls and live where he cannot be seen, touched, or bothered. From there, he has a lofty view of all below.

Have you ever thought of yourself as a spider? God wants us to learn that spiders and many other creatures are wise. We too can build our lives high above the world so we will not be touched or bothered by it. We do that by daily reading His Word and talking with Him. It is called edifying or building oneself up. Someday all those who have accepted Christ will live forever in the heavenly palace of the King. And the "mortgage" has already been paid by Christ. Do you still hate cobwebs? They surely are reminders of wise living, heavenly palaces, and that all of it is "free."

Dear God, I want to live high above the world around me. I want to be wise because You are leading me. Please help me to study and meditate today even while I feel busy so that the "world" won't tear me down. Thank You, Lord Jesus. Amen.

Rumpled Ruffles

Doilies

In the same way, you wives, be submissive to your own husbands so that even if any of them are disobedient to the word, they may be won without a word by the behavior of their wives, as they observe your chaste and respectful behavior. And let not your adornment be merely external—braiding the hair, and wearing gold jewelry, or putting on dresses; but let it be the hidden person of the heart, with the imperishable quality of a gentle and quiet spirit, which is precious in the sight of God.

—I Peter 3:1–4

Having received my credentials in interior decorating during the Middle Ages, I still love doilies. These frail, dainty, hand-crocheted doilies that ruffle under every lamp base, vase, and knick-knack are still part of my décor. While doilies do look so nice, they serve an even greater service. They cover scratches, water rings, and gouges in aging furniture.

The real problem with doilies is that they have to look really good in order to be used. Setting cold pizza crust and sweaty soda glasses on them just makes them go limp. I recently decided, during one of those insane cleaning sprees, to wash and starch all of my doilies. How stiff should starch be to make a doily ruffle stand up? Let me tell you, a bowl of cold oatmeal is thinner than starch for doilies! After dunking doilies for ten minutes, my fingers were so stuck together I had to use hot water and a vegetable brush to remove just the first layer of starch.

A few hours later, I removed these little white, lacy boards from the clothesline. Have you ever tried to iron plywood? *Sprinkle. Sprinkle.* Yes, they were beginning to take shape—not a doily shape, but some shape. In the meantime, the iron became crusted with starch, and the ironing board cover now matches the board—stiff! The next week I answered an ad for a lady who takes in ironing. Not even asking a price, I gave her this bag of mangled lace. If they cannot be saved, at least they will have a good home!

Doilies are just ornaments in our homes. They could even be called ornaments for the ornaments. How unnecessary they are. By comparison, our lives are filled with ornaments. We buy the latest styles in clothing, change hairstyles, endure permanents, plucked eyebrows, shaved legs, and even pierce our ears, all for the sake of appearances. Improving our appearance is fine, but it must not take precedence over improving our spiritual being. Do we spend as much time on our spiritual beauty as we do on our personal appearance or the adorning of our homes?

Today is the day to put away some of the old "doilies" in our lives. Instead, replace those with some love, patience, kindness, "... the imperishable quality of a gentle and quiet spirit ..." Now, what is the value of your new "doily"? Even to your family and friends, the change will be noticeable. They will see you as dear, satisfying, and valuable. But in the sight of God, your heart and your spirit, will be seen as "precious."

Dear Father, I know that a right spirit in me will never be out of style with You. I know it is not how I appear on the outside but what You see on the inside of me that counts. I so want to present You to those around me by being the woman in Your Word; I want that gentle and quiet spirit. I want to be that woman who can win others, "... without a word." I cannot do it on my own, so I am asking for Your help. Teach me today how to have your Spirit. Amen.

Sahara Bound

Humidifier

O God, Thou art my God; I shall seek Thee earnestly; my soul thirsts for Thee, my flesh yearns for Thee, in a dry and weary land where there is no water.

—Psalms 63:1

"Behold, days are coming," declares the Lord God, "when I will send a famine on the land, not a famine for bread or a thirst for water, but rather for hearing the words of the Lord. And people will stagger from sea to sea, and from the north even to the east; they will go to and fro to seek the word of the Lord, but they shall not find it."

—Amos 8:11–12

When the furnace clicks on in the fall, so does static electricity. You are probably more familiar with static electricity in dryers. Static electricity in the home is a monumental problem to deal with unless you have an adequate humidifier. Without humidity, every carpet, article of clothing, and human body becomes electrified and can be considered a lethal weapon.

Because our central heat used to be wood and we had only a small humidifier, static electricity abounded in our home. The favorite use for this was sheer treachery. My children shuffled up to me each time they wanted my attention, raking their little feet across the carpet. Then, *zap!* They would tap my hand or face and give me a shock. This was not the worst. Our poor unsuspecting dog had electrified hair after they did the same thing to her, except they touched her on her wet nose. Retaliation is easy though. When the phone would ring and it was for one of them (it was *always* for them), I merely shuffled around a few steps and got my revenge when I handed them the receiver.

A little water in our air can make all the difference. Once the humidifier places some moisture in the dry air, things return to normal. It is as if my carpet was beach sand just begging for some water to restore its vitality.

Our soul could be compared to those dry carpets. We become thirsty for God's love, God's Word, and God's Spirit. God promises in His Word to pour His Spirit into our lives if we just ask for it. He promises to "humidify" us.

Though the words in Amos are directed to the children of Israel, we can apply them today. Have you noticed a thirst in people for a meaning to life, a reason for living, a way to bring morality back to our country? They are thirsting for God. They are thirsting as never before to hear the Good News of Christ's precious gift, Himself.

Our souls should be like a dry carpet, ever desiring more of God's Spirit to saturate it. We can allow God to do that for us and we can be a "humidifier" in the lives of other people. Determine that today with God's help, you will begin to "humidify" your home with God's love. As this humidity spreads to your community, you can begin sharing that Christ can bring meaning to people's lives, a reason for living, and a set of standards that makes that living worthwhile.

O dear God, I am thirsty for your Spirit to drench me with Your love. As You pour it into my heart, help me to share it with everyone around me. I want to be as "moisture-refreshing" to all those who meet me today. Please bring me "dry" souls to help. I pray in the name of Jesus. Amen.

"Even when freshly washed and relieved of all obvious confections, children tend to be sticky."

Fran Lebowitz

C.S.I.
Fingerprints

Suddenly the fingers of a man's hand emerged and began writing opposite the lamp stand on the plaster of the wall of the king's palace, and the king saw the back of the hand that did the writing. (Please read the entire chapter.)

—Daniel 5:5

If you have been a homemaker for any length of time, you have become familiar with fingerprints. If you are a mother, you are personally waging a war against them! According to my calculations, a woman could practically take on a part-time job in exchange for the time she spends yearly washing off fingerprints.

Let's put our math to work. (Haven't you always hated those story problems?) A good example would be my sister. She has six children. At ten fingerprints per child, they have the capability of sixty fingerprints. Being conservative, let's estimate that each child leaves only one set of fingerprints per week or a collective total of 420 fingerprints per week. Multiplied by fifty-two weeks a year, that equals 21,840 fingerprints per year. If each child lives at home for eighteen years, my sister washed off a grand total of 393,120 fingerprints by the time those kids graduated. And I'm complaining? Having three children, my work was cut in half or only 196,560 fingerprints in those eighteen years! Phew! I feel better.

Three hard facts were omitted in the previous observations. First, the size of a fingerprint changes with the years. They start out with baby toddling prints and end up the size of a dinner plate. Second, the elevation of the fingerprint changes with the years. While toddler prints are near the floor, a growing teenager's challenge is to post their print above every doorway or on every ceiling in the house. Third, the texture of the fingerprint changes through the years. There's a vast difference between scrubbing off animal-gooey-crackers and axle grease or motor oil.

In Daniel, a man's hand appeared and wrote "on the plaster of the wall of the king's palace…" God didn't leave just a fingerprint, but he left a message on the wall. He spoke with finality to Belshazzar. Both his kingly reign and his life were finished and neither was pleasing to God.

Though God doesn't go through our homes leaving messages on the walls, He does leave some very definite messages in His Word. Like fingerprints, these messages change size applying to the young and old, large and small. Like fingerprints, they elevate themselves through the years as we mature as Christians and seek to understand His Word. Like fingerprints, they change texture, fitting different circumstances and speaking to different people. Like fingerprints, God's messages at times can be annoying because they bring us under conviction for sin in our lives. But like fingerprints, His Word reminds us of where we have been, where we are going, how much we have grown or need to grow, and that someday we will be mature in Christ.

Have you washed off any good fingerprints lately? Watch how big, how high, and how tough those fingerprints are. And then, remember how big, how high, and how tough God's love is for you!

O dear God, I am reminded today by those messy fingerprints of Your perfect love for me. I am reaching to remove some of them just as I desire to reach out and understand Your Word.

Help me to grow; help me to feel Your love for me. I love You and thank You for Jesus. Amen.

My Living Room/Family Room Journal

"I promise to work on this room and not take on the organization of any other room until this living room/family room is ready to greet my family and friends with warmth and hospitality."

1. Circle or name the three major problems in your living room or family room, prioritizing them with numbers.

   - Storage of magazines, newspapers, etc.
   - Lack of end tables or coffee table
   - Storage of CDs or DVDs
   - No storage space for blankets or throws
   - Arrangement of furniture
   - Room used for too many purposes (example: computer, study, toys, etc.)
   - Bookcases full and overflowing
   - Other:

____

____

2. Because I know God wants me to help my family enjoy time together, as well as showing friendship to others, I am asking God for His customized solution to do the following:

____

____

____

3. The Scripture that has encouraged me to organize this living room/family room is the following:

____

____

____

4. In order to complete my prioritized tasks, the supplies that I will need are the following:

   - Three containers for Trash, Donate, Save
   -
   -
   -
   -

(This is a good time to read and follow along with "It's Time to Organize That Living Room/Family Room.")

5. (*To be completed after your living room/family room organizing job is completed.)*
   I see that God helped me accomplish organizing this living room/family room. My feelings about the use of this room are now (include today's date):

____

____

____

____

6. My *one year later* journal entry about this room is (include the date):

____

It's Time to Organize That

Living Room/Family Room

Having observed and prayed about this room, I am sure you have analyzed how you want this room to look and how you want to improve the use of this area of your home. Get ready to buy paint because we are about to clear the clutter. Let's put on some jeans, push back the sofa, and dig in!

Again, start out with those three containers: Trash, Donate, Save.

Before beginning, step back and look at this room as if you were a guest just entering your home. Look high. Look low. What catches your eye? Clutter? Before organizing anything, gather all clutter that has been deposited by family members. Bag each individual's items and distribute them to the responsible parties. Once you have removed all *visible clutter*, let's evaluate a bit before actually working.

Think Before You Start

What will be the uses you want for this room? Write them down and be *committed* to those uses only. Why did the clutter gather in the room? Is it poor habits or is there no place to properly store *necessary items* for the living room? What items do you need to keep in this room? Your personal list of *necessary items* may differ from mine, but *do make a list.*

You will probably need some of these items:

- A place to store the daily newspaper
- Coasters to protect furniture
- A magazine holder

- A drawer or storage unit for remote controls for electronics
- A unit to store CDs and DVDs
- A sturdy, attractive basket to store blankets or throws.

Working from one side of the room in a circle may be the best plan of attack. Begin that "Circle Organization," leaving only what you find *necessary* for the *uses of that room.*

Front Door

If your front door opens into the living room, this is the perfect spot to begin your "Circle Organization," evaluating your room as if you were entering for the first time. *Go outside.* Come in, and do a thorough viewing of all the areas of the room from the perspective of a guest's vantage point. Do you have a rug to wipe wet shoes on? Is there a closet or coat rack handy? Is there anything that makes the guest feel your home is quiet, composed, happy, relaxed? Or do you sense messiness, noise, confusion? Identify with certainty what it is that gives the wrong impressions. Correct it, or remove it. Perhaps it is a table stacked with papers for school or jackets strewn on hooks. Remember that you are identifying how you *want* to use this room, and your goal is to make that happen. Now let's move into the living room and keep going.

End Tables and Storage Areas

Evaluate your storage possibilities in end tables and/or coffee tables. Should you purchase additional furniture to help contain the clutter? Do you have a place to contain your newspapers and magazines? If not, find something... even a basket will do until you have time to purchase what really works. If you already have a storage area for these, empty it and keep only today's paper and this month's magazines in it. Commit to keeping only this amount of material in the future.

Keep coasters and remotes within reach, not scattered all over. There are several designs to help contain these: a pretty little basket, crock, short vase, anything that compliments your room will do. The key here is to *contain* them while keeping it attractive.

CDs and DVDs

Even if you already have storage units for these, it is time to purge unused CDs and DVDs. When you have sorted all of them, take stock of how many you have, figure out *how many you will allow yourself to store* at any given time, and buy new wall hanging or stand-alone storage units. This way the clutter from them will be up off the floor, and it will be easier to read the titles. In the future, when purchasing new CDs or DVDs, remove or donate older ones, keeping your quantity limits in mind.

Book Cases

So many people have beautiful book cases loaded with books, magazines, and wonderful materials that are *never* read. Is this your situation? If so, be painfully honest, and donate the literature you no longer look at except when you dust the jackets. Unless a book has a sentimental value or high monetary value or is *useful,* it needs to go. No one wants your old high school or college books, and you can give away all those old romance novels. Use the shelf space for some family photos, photo albums, or to display memorabilia that can actually be enjoyed.

Furniture

Now that you have evaluated and stored all the smaller items of your room, you are ready to pull that furniture into the picture you have in mind for the use of this room. Remember that one of the goals of organizing your home was to have more guests into it, to entertain friends. Arrange the furniture in a good conversational grouping. If you do not feel talented at this, get a friend to help you create a new arrangement.

Trash, Donate, Save

Again, throw the trash away and donate the items ASAP without retrieving anything back into your household.

Sort the "save" items by taking them to the proper rooms and giving them to family members to place in their personal areas.

When you have completed organizing your living room/family room, take time to *praise and thank the Lord.*

Give Credit to the Lord

Dear Lord, You own this house and all that is in this entire world. I am just using it until You call me home. Lord, You know I want to use my home to warmly welcome family, friends, and visitors. Thank You for giving me the courage to eliminate a lot of clutter and organize the rest. Please help me to have the courage to invite people here to spend time with them and get to know them. I want to show them Your love, even here on this sofa, using this room for Your glory. I pray again in the name of Jesus. Amen.

Now go back a few pages and complete your *Living Room/Family Room Journal.*

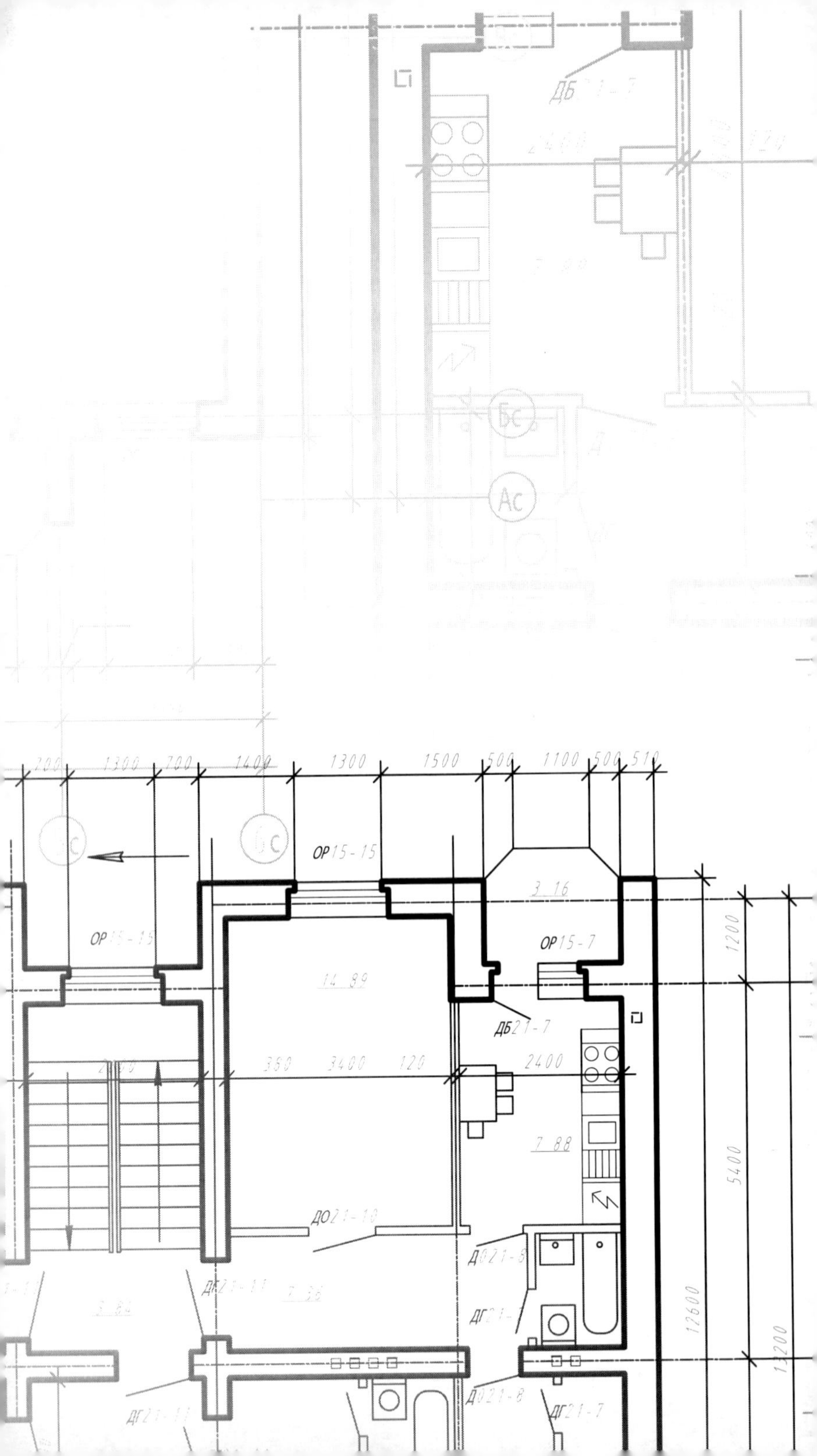
200
1300
700
1400
1300
1500
500
1100
500
510
ОР15-15
ОР15-15
3.16
ОР15-7
14.89
ДБ21-7
360
3400
120
2400
7.88
ДО21-10
ДО21-8
ДГ21-11
ДГ21-7
ДО21-8
ДГ21-11
ДГ21-7
1200
5400
12600
13200

Mattress Lumps and Clothing Clumps

The Bedroom

It's great that guests cannot see into every corner of the house because anyone seeing into the bedrooms might be horrified. Bedrooms seem to be the "clutter-gatherers" of the house. Can we really rest in a mess? Is our mess causing stress and time delays in the mornings? God Himself rested on the seventh day, so rest must be important to God. Let's look at some interesting thoughts from His Word and begin praying over our bedrooms. We need to bring order to our closets, our beds, and our "sanctuary" of the home.

Dear Jesus, it's been so easy to leave the mess in my bedroom because no one sees it... except You. Please help me appreciate the wonderful clothing You have provided for me. Help me to share what I no longer need, and guide me to form new habits of caring for my clothing. I want to create a restful room that reflects my respect for everything in this room. I thank You even before I begin because I know You care how I live. I pray this in Jesus' name. Amen.

Rockin' Mama

The Long Night

But he himself went a day's journey into the wilderness, and came and sat down under a juniper tree; and he requested for himself that he might die, and said, "It is enough, now, O Lord, take my life, for I am not better than my fathers." And he lay down and slept under a juniper tree; and behold there was an angel touching him and he said to him, "Arise, eat." Then he looked and behold there was at his head a bread cake baked on hot stones, and a jar of water. So he ate and drank and lay down again. And the angel of the Lord came again a second time and touched him and said, "Arise, eat, because the journey is too great for you."

—I Kings 19:4–7

I found this interesting entry in my journal from those days as a young mother:

> He's better this morning, only a little fussiness and lack of appetite. How thankful I am that he is better today! I've been up all night with him. I would cry too if I were so little and so miserable. The fever lasted through the night then rose and peaked and broke about 5 a.m. His congestion kept him from sleeping soundly in a lying position, so I cradled him on my shoulder for several hours of fitful sleep between fussing. It's been a long night, and now it is morning. My husband needs breakfast, and the older children need lunches and clothes for school.
>
> They have all left for work and school now. It is just the baby and me again. There is so much work to do. Beds, dishes, laundry sit round about me screaming for attention but I am so tired, so drained.

How many times have we felt completely exhausted as a mother, as a woman? It is not just the physical exhaustion, but the mind feels drained as well. We just need to get some sleep! The man referred to in the verse above is Elijah, a prophet of God. Elijah must have felt more than drained when he was in the wilderness. In one day he built an altar, dug a trench, gathered wood, cut up a bullock, slew the prophets of Baal, then ran a day's distance into the wilderness to escape Jezebel. And I thought *I* was tired! God ministered to Elijah with sleep and food and he was refreshed. God ministers to us, too, through sleep to keep our body healthy and strong just as he ministered to Elijah. God created sleep because He knew our bodies need it.

Have you been caring for your family and missing your rest? Sleep, Mother. God designed it as a blessing for you.

Dear God, my body and my mind are often so tired. It is so good for me to remember that You know how I feel and that You care for my body and health as well as my spiritual being. Please give me just the rest I need to carry on the work that is needed for today. Help me to discern necessary work from what I think should be done. I need Your hand upon me to make even this decision. Thank You, Jesus, for caring for me. Amen.

"If truth is beauty, how come no one has her hair done in the library?"

Lily Tomlin

The Great Cover-Up
Making Beds

Blessed are those whose lawless deeds have been forgiven, and whose sins have been covered.

—Romans 4:7

Being too tall for almost any bed he has ever slept in, my husband must hold the world's record for "Most Sheets Pulled Loose in a Lifetime." It's a foot thing. First, the top sheet must be lifted with the feet at the bottom corner until it is pulled out. Then the blankets follow. Next comes a complete night of wrestling with said sheets and blankets until the morning "crumple" takes shape. Then, each morning we automatically, mechanically begin to make it all back up. It is as if the day's beginning depended on it. After all, we expect to get back into a smooth, clean bed each night so we can begin this process all over again.

Did you ever think of how much it takes to make up a bed just so we can lie down and sleep? First, some like to encase their mattress in a plastic mattress covering. Next, we pull on the mattress pad to protect the mattress and give us a smooth cushion under the sheets. Then, of course, the snugly fitted sheet follows and then, the matching flat sheet. Blankets are added, maybe even piled, for warmth. The pillows are zipped into their pillow covers then covered again with pretty cases that match our sheets. Finally, we cover all these covers with the final covering, the bedspread, or comforter.

How happy I am that all the things I've done to displease God are not like my bed, requiring many coverings to hide them. And the "covering" for my sins is not routinely soiled or deteriorated needing laundering or replacement. Christ covered them once and for all with His precious blood, never to be seen or remembered again by Him. His blood is perfect, spotless, and does not need reapplication or replacing on the same sins. Furthermore, He has provided this "covering" for the sins we will commit in the future. Oh, that my sheets could expand, and I would never need to buy bedding again.

He has fitted us for our perfect rest in Him with His perfect covering. May we claim it for ourselves and share the good news of it this day with others.

Thank You for letting me make beds today, Lord. Thank You for "making my bed," for covering me with Yourself. In the name of Jesus, I pray. Amen.

Hanger Hideout
Closets

Thou art my hiding place; thou dost preserve me from trouble; thou dost surround me with songs of deliverance.

—Psalms 32:7

Now, don't get me wrong. I like closets. I think closets are great to have. It's just that sometimes they are so full the doors won't shut and the clutter inside is all jumbled together.

My closets seem to be what you would call a "catch all." The kids thought the word closet was synonymous with the words "hamper," "toy box," "shoe rack," "basement," and "wastepaper can"! Is company coming? Hide the basket of unfolded laundry in the closet. Have an extra coat to hang up? Throw it into the closet. Have a new clumsy appliance to store with no cupboard space? Put it in the closet. Those kids learned from the pro! And sometimes, I feel like hiding in the closet myself instead of sorting everything out and cleaning it up.

What a great hiding place we have in our God! He hides our every sin, He hides us from troubles, and He hides us from the evil one. Yes, we need to hide sometimes.

Do you have a trouble, a worry, a grief, an unconfessed sin, a heavy temptation? Go to your "closet," and hide yourself there. Put all those things on the shelf or hang them up. Name each one as you toss out those problems: selfishness, disappointment, frustrations, jealousy, envy, bitterness, anger. In the shelter of that "closet," there is light; no clutter, only serenity.

Aren't closets great after all?

O dear Jesus, I feel a need to be hidden in You today. You see all the burdens that I am carrying and I want to ask You to lift them off my shoulders and put them away on the "shelf" of Your heart. Will You close me out from the world today by helping my mind meditate on Your Word all day? Will You lift my spirits by helping me to imagine myself closed in a small place with You? I need Your quietness, Your peace, Your touch. Thank You, Jesus. Amen.

Citizen's Arrest
Tags

Because by the works of the Law no flesh will be justified in His sight; for through the Law comes the knowledge of sin . . . For we maintain that a man is justified by faith apart from works of the Law.

—Romans 3:20, 28

Every housewife has a little "imp" in her. I do! It comes out most whenever I see a fluffy new pillow that is trailing a long white tag reading, "Under Penalty of Law this tag must not be removed. . . ." You have seen these tags on several types of household items.

Have you ever felt a surge of power as you tear off that "Under Penalty of Law" tag? I just tore one off my rocking chair this morning, set it aside, and have waited for the authorities to come to my door. It's almost time for dinner, and still no officers. Who would report this? Is there a sensor at the factory that goes off when the tag is ripped free? Instead of fear, I am feeling quite smug that I have gotten away with it!

Yet, I am reminded of this verse in Romans 3:20 that says, "Because by the works of the Law no flesh will be justified in His sight; for through the Law comes the knowledge of sin." The law is our condemnation. But Christ, because He loved us, paid our penalty through His death on the cross and now is resurrected and ascended into heaven. He is our justification or vindication or exoneration or our "bail money" as Romans 3: 28 continues to show, "For we maintain that man is justified by faith apart from works of the Law."

I am so thankful that God at His great throne will not have to attach a tag on me reading "Under Penalty of Law." But instead will label me "Justified, Vindicated,

Exonerated, Bailed Out, and Acquitted in Christ." Start looking for these labels, remembering *your* justification is in Him every time you find one.

O Heavenly Father, thank You so much for the knowledge that we are no longer under the penalty of the Law. Thank You for Jesus Who has paid my penalty for sin, and I have a new label, a new name: Forgiven. I am thanking You in the name of Jesus, my Savior. Amen.

Our first step is to seek God's will—then do it. We must know and do that which He has already revealed to us before He will give further guidance. The Scriptures tell us, "Your words are a flashlight to light the path ahead of me, and keep me from stumbling" (Psalms 119:105LB). We need to use God's flashlight constantly.[3]

Nancy Dorner

Body Mass vs. Screws
The Handrail

God is our refuge and strength, a very present help in trouble.

—Psalms 46:1

Uphold me that I may be safe, that I may have regard for Thy statutes continually.

—Psalms 119:117

For several years there was no handrail on our upstairs stairway. I never really missed having one except that I do have a problem: stumbling. Corners and stairways have always been the causes of bruised shoulders and twisted ankles for me. Well, no more.

With the installation of the new handrail, our family made several remarkable discoveries. First, by following the handrail, a flight of stairs can be easily maneuvered even when someone turns off the lights leaving you in total darkness. We will not name names! Second, by forcefully pulling on the handrail, a girl can bound up at least three stairs at a time when in pursuit of an unlocked diary. Third, by putting his full weight on the handrail and lunging forward, a boy can jump down no less than a full flight of stairs in a single leap while escaping with said diary in hand. Fourth, a handrail can only take so much stress before the screws pop out of the wall and it becomes a health hazard. I was the next person to use it. Lesson number five, do not ever trust a handrail!

As my husband resets the screws in that handrail, I am reminded how God wants to be a handrail in our lives. He desires to be our guide, in sunny times as well as in dark times. He wants to support us, hold us up from all our cares, and aid us in our escape from life's stumbling blocks.

How I know God would never fail as this handrail did! He can't, and He won't! He is omnipresent, omniscient, and omnipotent. *He will never fail us!* The next time you use your handrail, imagine leaning on God and feel His strong support. Then the next time lean harder, and the next time harder yet, and the next time…

Precious Father, I see You today as the support in my daily life. You know the circumstances I face right now. I need Your strength. By Your Spirit, keep Your Word fresh on my mind today that I may draw encouragement and direction. Thank You for Your constant faithfulness to me. Amen.

The Rise and Fall

Stairs

My foot stands on a level place; in the congregations I shall bless the Lord.

—Psalms 26:12

Teach me Thy way, O Lord and lead me in a level path, because of my foes.

—Psalms 27:11

There aren't too many spots in the house as hard to clean or keep clean as the stairs. But why are vacuum cleaner hoses only four feet long and the cord only six feet long when an average stairway is ten feet long? Being blessed with a two-story home with a basement, I have become very familiar with stairs.

Some stairways are built with nice, wide stairs, evenly spaced. But I don't find those when I am out. I seem to find the ones that have one runner smaller than my foot and the bottom step is at least two inches higher than the rest of the stairway. *Thud!* And, have you ever tried to carry a laundry basket over those three-inch steps at the coin laundry? First, you cannot see it with the basket in the way, and secondly, it is just the right height to catch your toe and send you flying spread-eagled toward the change machine. I speak from experience.

But two sets of steps stand out vividly in my memory. The first set was on a school bus in my senior year of high school. With the agility of a gazelle, I tripped going up the steps and removed half of the skin on both shins just before the senior prom. The second set got me a few years later in an apartment we rented. Our dear and meticulous Latvian landlord painted my back, outdoor steps one afternoon without telling me. While taking out the garbage, I remember touching the top step, feeling a flying sensation, and landing on the concrete, looking up at the sky. My pride was more damaged than my body that time.

Have you ever thought of how much we need safe, even footing in our homes and in our lives? God provides for His children level, unshakable, secure ground. There is no variance in His Word, His love, this holy ground, this "even place."

Where have you placed your feet? Are you climbing, stumbling, and falling? Do you desire no stairways, no slippery spots, and no edges in life upon which to trip? As you climb or clean steps today, seek God. Plant your faith, your heart, your life on this even ground, this even "place." Enjoy "ranch-style" living!

My dear Heavenly Father, I claim the promise of living on level ground. I want to climb, to mature but I need Your steady support, Your unchanging sameness in my life. Please pick me up when I stumble and plant me on that flat place; keep my life steady. I thank You for this. Amen.

Dacron Duels

Pillows

For this we say to you by the word of the Lord, that we who are alive, and remain until the coming of the Lord, shall not precede those who have fallen asleep. For the Lord himself will descend from heaven with a shout, with the voice of the archangel, and with the trumpet of God; and the dead in Christ shall rise first. Then we who are alive and remain shall be caught up together with them in the clouds to meet the Lord in the air, and thus we shall always be with the Lord. Therefore, comfort one another with these words.

—I Thessalonians 4:15–18

New bed pillows are a rare purchase. A few years ago, my children needed new pillows, and I was happy the annual white sale made it possible to buy them. It was sheer joy to replace the old, flat pillows with fluffy new ones. The kids thought these were "neat," "great," and "groovy."

However, several mornings later I noticed that the boys' new pillows were on the floor, and the old wads of Dacron that used to be called their pillows were on the beds. I thought they had probably found the new ones were better weapons in a game they played called "kill your brother," so I just put them back on the beds. A few days later, I noticed both boys had the old pillows back on their beds, and the new pillows were stuffed in the toy box. That night I heard the complaints of, "They're too high; they hurt my neck," and, "They're just too fat," for the last time. I insisted they would never get used to them if they didn't use them. Furthermore, notice was given that the old pillows were not to be dragged out again unless we had company and were short of pillows. It was the new pillows or else!

The next few days opened my eyes. The old pillows weren't dragged out, but the new pillows were still found on the floor each morning. They preferred to sleep flat as boards rather than use those beautiful, new pillows. It was compromise time. From then on, both pillows were kept on the bed. One was for sleeping, and the other was considered a lethal weapon when those boys were in that room together. This was my reward for trying to bring a little comfort and softness into their lives!

Pillows have just that one purpose to us . . . comfort. They are to be soft uplifting cushions to rest our weary heads upon when we are at the end of a long day. How much like a pillow is Christ's promise to return someday soon to take us to be with Him forever. There's comfort in knowing that hard work, disappointments, death, illness, bills, and even children's fighting won't have to make us weary anymore. Ahead will be heaven, Christ, joy, light, and peace. Fluff your pillow tonight as you lie down, and remember the word "comfort." Then remember Christ's comfort to us; close your eyes, and rest in it.

Precious Father, I am weary so many times, and I long for the reminder of Your return. O God, I am looking forward to eternity with You, to being taken from the weights of life. Please remind me today of Your great promise to not leave me here but to return to take me to be with You. I long for that peaceful place with You. Thank You for this comfort. You are my "pillow." I pray in Christ's name. Amen.

Dust-Bunnies Uncaged
"Under"

Be gracious to me, O God, be gracious to me, for my soul takes refuge in Thee; and in the shadow of Thy wings I will take refuge, until destruction passes by.

—Psalms 57:1

He will cover you with His pinions, and under His wings you may seek refuge; His faithfulness is a shield and bulwark.

—Psalms 91:4

... How often I wanted to gather your children together, the way a hen gathers her chicks under her wings ...

—Matthew 23:37b

A house can generally be divided into two areas: an "upper" and an "under." The "upper" is the area from the standing housewife's eyeball upward. For short people like me, this is a large area, especially with nine and a half foot ceilings! I have come to believe that doorways, chandeliers, drapery rods, and ceiling fans are curses on mankind invented by men who were over nine feet tall!

The area known as the "under" is also large, starting from the housewife's nose downward. A person need not have keen eyesight to find the problems of "under" areas. Many a housewife's nose has discovered a dead mouse under the kitchen stove long before an eye saw it. How many bare feet under the table have found that one squishy slice of banana that flipped from the cereal bowl? How many fuzzy slippers have left the bedrooms with dust balls attached from under the bed?

We begin to get goose bumps when we think of all the "under" areas of the house. Have you looked lately under the refrigerator, under your dresser, under the washer and dryer, under the chest freezer, under the furnace, or worst of all, under the basement stairway? All of these areas hide junk, dust, and dirt. Nothing clean resides in the "under" areas.

Our lives are often like the hidden dust and dirt in the "under" areas. Our very best deeds are only as "filthy rags," dirt (Reference: Isaiah 64:6). But the adoring, sheltering love of Christ covers us under the shadow of His wing. Under that wing, we are protected, hidden from the world and the evil one, nestled safely as a chick with its mother. What a sanctuary is provided for us as we are hidden "under."

Bend down and check the "under" areas of your home right now. Thank the Lord for dust balls, food scraps, and whatever else you find. Thank Him that within your home lies an area to remind you that you are living in the best "under" area, under His precious wing.

My dear Father, I am looking today for areas to remind me that I am hidden under the shadow of Your wing. I feel I need that protection, a shelter from life's hurts and burdens right now. Please awaken my senses to feel Your presence. Amen.

My Bedroom Journal

"I promise to work on this room and not take on the organization of any other room until this bedroom, clothing, and closets are organized and the feeling of relaxation is felt when I enter it."

1. Circle or name three major problem areas in your bedroom, prioritizing them with numbers.

   - Clothes seldom hung up or put away
   - Closets too full, disorganized
   - Under-bed area full
   - Dressers too small
   - Atmosphere not restful (pillows, mattress, temperature, etc.)
   - Bedroom has too many uses (computer, work papers, gifts, etc.)
   - Arrangement of furniture
   - Other:

   ____

   ____

2. Because I know my rest is important to God, my prayer for God's customized solution is the following:

   ____

   ____

   ____

3. The Scripture that has encouraged me to organize this bedroom is the following:

   ____

   ____

4. In order to complete my prioritized tasks, the supplies that I will need are the following:

   - Three containers for Trash, Donate, Save
   -
   -
   -
   -

(This is a good time to read and follow along with "It's Time to Organize That Bedroom.")

5. *(To be completed after your bedroom organizing job is finished.)*
   I see that God helped me accomplish organizing this bedroom. My feelings about this room are now (include today's date):

6. My *one year later* journal entry about this bedroom is (include the date):

It's Time to Organize That
Bedroom

You will find the bedroom(s) may be your toughest assignment because so much of what is stored here will have some sentimental value to you. Women tend to place a sentimental value on clothing worn on memorable occasions such as weddings, anniversaries, first dates, the honeymoon, bringing baby home from the hospital, the first job interview, shopping with the girls at the mall, or crying at a movie. We don't really need a reason to hold onto clothing; we just like clothing. This will be the time to *prayerfully* find the courage to *rationally* look at each item of clothing and purge all that you can.

After reading and praying over the Scriptures we already studied, you must sense that God is *interested* in your sleep, solitude, escape, and order. Strip the sheets off the bed, open the closet doors and let's go!

Get those three containers ready: Trash, Donate, Save. Let's start in the hidden parts of the bedroom first.

Closets

First, remove all the clothing from the closet. You may have the desire to evaluate each item as it is removed or you can first stack it and then evaluate how often you wear each garment. Be asking yourself if it fits well or how do you look in it. Don't wait for it to fit again or come back in style. Rule of thumb: if you have not worn it for a year, donate it. Are you listening? *Donate it!* If it *truly* has sentimental value, then put it in a sealed storage container labeled "Memorabilia" for later use. Just remember to control how *many* items you place sentimental value upon and decide to store.

I really could not part with the three dresses that I had worn to each of my children's weddings, but there was no reason for them to be stored in my closet. How could I sell them at a consignment shop or garage sale or donate them to a charity? I felt I would be discarding a part of my most precious memories. Laying them aside for one more day, I asked the Lord to give me His perspective on the value of these dresses and to not let me become "my own client," unable to throw away or give away clutter. My unique answer came as I looked at my sewing machine. Simple sewing is my best effort and I realized that I could create new memories for the next generation by preserving these few garments. I placed them in a small, sealed storage box knowing that I will be able to use fancy pieces of them to make the back of ring bearer's pillows as gifts for my grandchildren. These have taken virtually no space in the box in the attic, they will serve as a bit of history someday when the grandchildren marry, and will have special meaning to three generations at a later date. This was a good reminder that memories are important to us and also to God. Customized answer received!

Second, before returning clothing to the closet, evaluate if you need or can afford a new closet storage unit. If it can be done, a new unit will help contain long clothing to short items to small undergarments in drawers and even shoes. Consider the purchase of a new unit. If you cannot afford one right now, use new shoe racks, new belt hangers, raise one small bar to create two tiers of shirts or blouses, and arrange some dividers for the top shelf of the closet so sweaters or sweatshirts can be stacked on the top without falling over. Also, *look up.* Is there wasted space in the top of the closet, above the shelf? Can another shelf be added? Also, can *hooks* be installed for robes or slacks that get more than one wearing? Consider all these possibilities as you design a new plan to store clothing.

Third, once you have decided on a new or old closet system, divide your *chosen* clothing into seasons. Usually just two seasons will do: summer and winter. If you are not able to store both seasons in your closet without bunching them, place one season's clothing in sealed storage units to be placed in another location. This could be a basement or attic or spare bedroom closet. Be sensitive to the temperatures and humidity at which you are storing the clothing.

Dressers

Let's start at the top and work down. Remove all the items on top of the dresser. After polishing the top, return only the items that are needed on a daily basis. Perhaps you need a jewelry box, a small receptacle for keys and pocket items, and something pretty. Keep the top as clear and plain as possible. It will give you a feeling of *clean* to "declutter" it.

Let's move on to the drawers: Starting at the top, use one drawer for underwear, and add socks if possible. Again, purge down to what you *need.* If you have fourteen pairs of underpants and wash every few days, why store all of this? Keep about seven or eight pairs in the drawer and leave room for other small garments. Remember to group your clothing in drawers by *use.* For example, one drawer for underwear and socks, one for pajamas, one for shorts or work shirts, and one for better T-shirts. The amount of clothing in each area will depend on the size of the drawer. *Just use the drawers, and stop using the floor!*

Night Stands

You can find a little extra storage space in night stands or occasional tables in the bedroom. Use the extra drawers for small items that would be used at some time in the bedroom. For instance, a flashlight, headphones for a radio, an extra television remote, a special light bulb for reading lights, etc. would fit in a small drawer. If your night stands are open, this is a perfect place to store that extra book you intend to read before bed… someday. If you need heating pads or extra items to be kept handy to your bed, find space in these drawers to meet that need.

Hamper

Though hampers usually are best located in the bathroom, you will need to decide if placing one in the bedroom will avoid all those clothes ending up on the floor. Can it be placed between the bathroom and the bedroom? Make a plan to use more than one hamper if it will help. Some people find one in each bedroom helps keep clothes off the floor and are easy to gather at laundry time. Decide on a plan that works for you. You may have to experiment.

The Bed

We have saved the best for last. Let's start *under* the bed. Remove everything, and using those three favorite containers, sort it. Do not put anything back under the bed *unless* you are absolutely unable to store items elsewhere. Having the bed clear underneath, you are able to keep dust under control and the room has a better feeling of openness.

Where are you storing your linens for the bed? A linen closet is the ideal. Here again, sort out all unused linens, and donate them. A good rule of thumb is to keep two sets of sheets and one to two blankets for each bed. In colder climates, you may want a set of flannel sheets as well. Keep sheets and pillowcases in a neat stack. Or you may find it efficient to store the pillow cases folded into the sheets as a set.

If you do not have a linen closet or space in your bedroom closet and *really* do not have another space to store sheets and cases, you might consider making an exception to the storage of them under the bed. There are wonderful rolling under-the-bed storage units available and these seal well and keep items clean and protected. They would also be at your fingertips when you are ready to change the bedding. These should be the *only* items considered for under-the-bed storage.

Children's Bedrooms

Some rules begin to be broken when it comes to children's rooms, but you can use the listing above to organize these also. Just make a few adjustments.

Children's Bedroom Toys

Try to contain toys to one corner of the room. Have a shelving unit or a toy box to help *form the habit of picking up the toys at the end of each day.* Some larger, plastic drawer units fit easily into children's closets for storage of puzzles, small toys, small clothing, games, etc. Since children's clothing is shorter and smaller, the bottom of the closet is ideal to fit organizing units or perhaps even a dresser.

Here we *consider* breaking the under-the-bed rule also. If you find drawers that fit under the frame of the bed, by all means use these. Otherwise, many storage units will slide under, and they can provide just the right place for many games and toys that have multiple parts. Some toys are used very infrequently, and those would be ideal stored away under the bed.

Another possibility for under-the-bed storage would be the next-size-up storage bins for your children's clothing. It may be handier here and ready-for-use as growth or the change of seasons require.

Use this idea very sparingly. Don't get the kids used to pushing things under the bed to hide them. You want children to understand that their bedroom is a place of *rest,* not mess.

Hanging shoe storage bags are excellent for the smallest of children's necessities. Hair ribbons, barrettes, combs, brushes, small lotions, small toy parts that need attention, etc. can all fit into these pockets and can be seen easily. Hang these on the back of a door.

Children's Closets

I only address this separately because children tend to outgrow clothing so quickly, and when there are several children in the family, we don't want to purge or donate the clothes. But how do you begin to store all those clothes from child to child?

Start with considering *style.* If your children are several years apart, the clothing will look dated when the next child is ready to wear it, no matter how expensive and good it is now. If there is a large age gap, consider selling really good children's clothing at a consignment store.

Next, consider the *quality* of the clothing you are tempted to store. Most jeans can show a lot of wear and should be donated. There is probably no use in saving items that are only the quality of "play clothes."

Third, *if* you have some items you really must store, put them into containers marking them BOY—size 2 or GIRL—size 8, etc.

Again, use sealed storage units to get maximum protection for the garments. If you have several units, consider the under-the-bed storage option above.

Use the organization of your children's rooms to teach good habits from an early age.

Children's Memorabilia

All children create new crafts and papers that they want to display or see. Look to the walls. Be sure to have a corkboard at their eye-level for those papers. Check out the new metallic paint that creates an area to use with magnets. Also, a new lower shelf will hold many items and keep the clutter off the floor and dresser. Respect their pride and their need to see their creations by making a way for them to keep these items neatly displayed in their rooms.

Older Teen to College-Age Rooms

Teens seem to be able to exist in floors covered with clothes and homework. Have a good talk with your teen, and ask how you can help them have less stress and live in a more sensible, not sterile, room. Can you supply them with a new closet unit? Consider using a new shelf for their CD player and CDs or some new baskets for homework. Get their input and color/style preferences. Then *shop and work together* reorganizing their new spaces.

They will take more interest and initiative if they feel they have been a part of this change.

For older children living away from home, you are the storage unit for their "shrine" of a bedroom. Tell them you are going to start *boxing* their belongings for them. Assure them that you will respectfully *not throw away anything or read their private papers.* Your job is not to sort their belongings, but to contain and preserve them. Label the boxes with their name only or a colored paper, possibly their favorite color, so they can find their belongings later. Super sticky notes now come in a large size, enabling contents to be easily listed. Their empty room or part of a room will serve to move the family forward, yet leave their belongings intact, awaiting their personal attention. Store everything in temperature and humidity controlled areas. Remember, *be respectful.*

Give Credit to the Lord

When you have worked through even one bedroom, *take time to praise and thank the Lord.*

O dear God, I am so thankful for the wonderful bedroom(s) You have given me. I thank You for the rest that I will have here. I am thankful for the gracious spirit You have blessed me with and the ability to donate all these items to those who need them. I look forward to having many wonderful hours in this bedroom and being able to have mornings that are less stressful because our clothes are now in order. Help me to develop and keep good habits to care for all these blessings You have given to me. Amen.

Now go back a few pages and complete your *Bedroom Journal.*

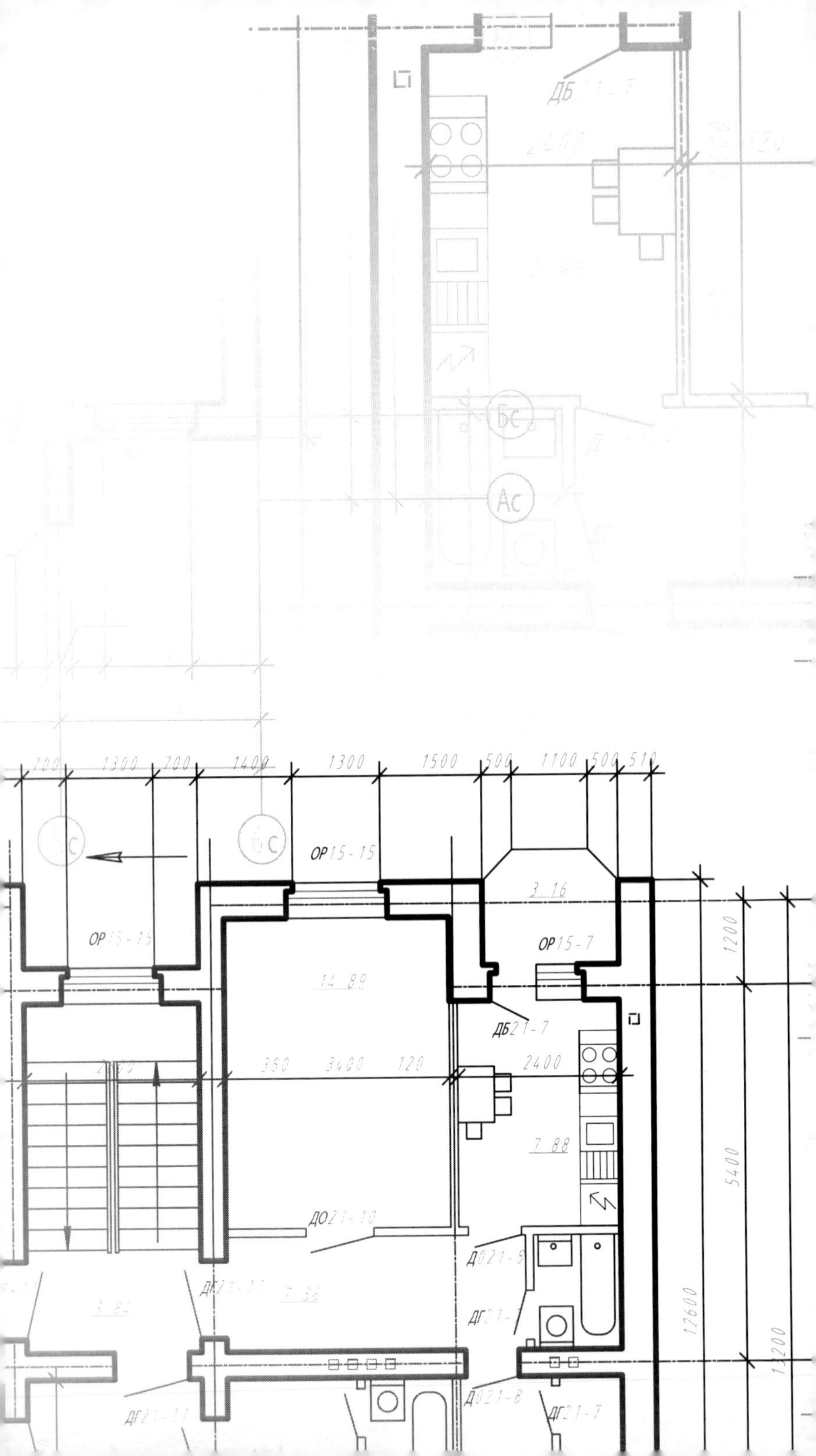

700
1300
700
1400
1300
1500
500
1100
500
510
Бс
ОР15-15
ОР15-15
3.16
ОР15-7
1200
14.89
ДБ21-7
360
3400
120
2400
7.88
5400
ДО21-10
ДО21-8
ДГ21-11
ДГ21-7
12600
13200
ДГ21-11
ДО21-8
ДГ21-7

Soap on a Rope, the Only Thing Hung Up in My Bathroom

The Bathroom

This vital room gets us off to work in the morning and refreshes us at the end of the day. So many items in this room can be reminders of God at work. It is important to take time to consider how we not only can improve our bathroom storage, but make our bathroom a pleasant place to be.

What bathroom chapter would be complete without a devotional about the toilet? From this delicate subject to chapped hands and hardened caulking, this chapter covers the nuts and bolts of organizing. *Organizing is all about meeting the needs of the family.* Safety is featured in the storage of medications and cleaning supplies. When we hang up the last towel, the Lord will be thanked for His special help in a most "hostile environment."

Dear Lord, You know it is hard to pray over something like a bathroom, but You also know that I am asking for Your help in every room of my house. Please help me to organize this room so that it will not only be clean, but be as refreshing to use as the water that flows from the shower. Only You can help me have the energy and wisdom to do this. I thank You for what You are going to do through me. Amen.

Reflection of Perfection

Mirrors

And He is the image of the invisible God, the first-born of all creation.

—Colossians 1:15

The only thing as painfully accurate as a photograph is a mirror. Immediate wealth awaits the inventor of a "lying mirror." No wrinkles, warts, bulges, bags, blemishes, droops, or sags would be seen in that mirror. Only youthful figures, soft skin, clear eyes, and perfect hair would be reflected. Imagine the market for such a mirror!

If invented, this should be the only mirror allowed in bathrooms. Getting up in the morning would be so pleasant. But a few things would be difficult if the mirror only reflected perfection instead of truth. It would be impossible for men to shave; no stubble would ever appear. It would not be necessary to comb your hair; it would look combed and set already. Children could snap toothpaste at it, write on it when it got steamed up, put fingerprints all over it, and still it would never appear dirty or distorted. Even the wicked queen in Snow White could never have wished for a mirror like this. But by using this fantasy mirror, everyone would leave the house with messy hair, food in their teeth, and a dirty face.

Did you realize there has been a perfect "mirror" already created? Christ was just such a mirror sent by the Great Inventor, God the Father. Christ was reflecting the invisible God throughout all of His life. He reflected God's love and concern. He reflected patience and understanding. He reflected power and authority. He reflected

His Father. Christ was that perfect reflection of God's eternal love for mankind.

As you look into a mirror today and see your reflection, think about Christ's reflection. He wants you to see His real image and to know Him as He really is. He deserves your praise, adoration, and worship for what He reflects. Then consider your own reflection to those around you. Have you emptied yourself so you can reflect Christ? You can be that inventor! You can create a mirror that only reflects perfection. Only you can reflect a perfect Christ to the world around you.

My dear Father, I do give You all my adoration and praise today. I am reminded that You have created all things, You are holding them together, You have created me, and You are "holding me together" also. Your Son has reflected You to me, and You are love. Oh dear God, use me to reflect You to all those around me. Please make me the mirror of You to them. Thank You. Amen.

Cement Clone

Grout

For they had not gained any insight from the incident of the loaves, but their heart was hardened.

—Mark 6:52

If you have a bathtub or shower, you know a little about grout. If you have ceramic tile or slate, you know a lot about grout. If you have a bathtub, shower, ceramic tile, and slate, you are an expert on the subject of grout.

This little bit of hardened gel in cracks has been a thorn in the housewife's flesh ever since it was invented. It is one of those products that could only have been invented by a man! No woman would ever choose to put up a wall full of little squares and fill in all the cracks so they had to be cleaned with a toothbrush! You remember what grout looks like. It's that black, furry stuff in the shower stall that used to be white. Or it could be the brown, gritty stuff in the entry that used to be pearl gray.

Grout does have one redeeming quality though. It cannot be penetrated by water or dirt or even with screwdrivers or paring knives. Did you ever have it crack and need replacing? The first time that happened in my tub, I broke three screwdrivers, two paring knives, and bent one nut pick removing a six inch section. The next time it needs replacing, I think I will rent a jack-hammer, and I probably can have it done in thirty-five minutes. The tub may look a little pitted where I drop the drill bits, but I will get every piece of it out.

God can almost compare our hearts to grout. When we first begin our personal relationship with Him, our heart is soft and tender to His love and leading. As time goes by, we grow careless, and our hearts may become dull and insensitive. Finally, we fail to recognize what great wonders He does every day for us. We fail to look for His presence. We become hardened.

In this Scripture passage, notice that immediately after Christ had performed the miracle of feeding five thousand people from just a little boy's lunch, He sent the disciples into the boat to go to Bethsaida. They took their eyes and thoughts off Him and immediately forgot that Christ was God in the flesh, that nothing could have harmed them. They had seen with their own eyes the wonders of Jesus' power, yet gained nothing in their spirit. How sad for the disciples! How sad for us that this is the nature of man!

As you clean the grout in your home, think about the condition of your own heart. Is it covered with mildew or dirt? Has it "hardened"? Is it still soft and pliable, seeking God's very best for your life? By reading God's Word, get out that old "grout" and put in a soft, new replacement. Let God mold it into His perfect pattern for you.

Dear precious Father, I want to be different from Your disciples, yet I know that my heart is the very same as theirs. Help me to see Your power, Your love, and be changed by it. Help me to soften my own heart by reading Your Word. I commit to that, O God. Thank You for giving me Jesus. Amen.

A Slippery Subject
Soap

I testify to everyone who hears the words of the prophecy of this book: if anyone adds to them, God shall add to him the plagues which are written in this book; and if anyone takes away from the words of the book of this prophecy, God shall take away his part from the tree of life and from the holy city, which are written in this book.

—Revelation 22:18–19

Soap comes in many forms. What would we do without the handy powdered and liquid soap we can use for our laundry? How could we wash our hands without a bar of soap that is shaped to exactly fit our soap dish? One squirt of liquid soap and our dishwater is ready. Throw in a bubble bath bead, and we have bubbles in which to lounge. What man could give up his shaving lather or hand cleaner for the shop?

Soap not only comes in many forms, it can be used to solve some tough problems around the house. When winter comes bringing sticky jacket zippers, out comes the bar of soap. Squeaking hinges, sticking doors and dresser drawers, and swollen windows are only a few areas that can be made to move with a good old bar of soap! If you are a gardener, you can use a bit of liquid soap in a sprayer to rid your garden plants of aphids. And how many children have enjoyed carving a bar of soap into a special gift for a mother or grandmother?

Soap causes me to think of God's Word, the Holy Bible. Though it does not come in different forms, some folks experiment with it, trying to change it to suit their liking. Oh, some water it down, liquefying it, and just ooze it all over while others grind it all up, powder it, and make it as a dust, as nothing. Still others dehydrate it and consolidate it, leaving out bits and pieces and soon have a smaller, neat little bar. God's Word says in Revelation 22:18–19 that we are to neither add to nor take away from His Book.

God's Word, like soap, has a seemingly unlimited list of uses. It is a balm to the grieving heart, hope to the despairing, a convicting light into the sinner's heart, a chastisement to the erring Christian, a parental guide, a newlywed's home plan, a retiree's satisfaction in old age, a child's guide to obedience, and on and on and on. So don't powder it, don't dehydrate it, and don't liquefy it. We can take it and use it in its already perfect form to meet all of our needs. The next time you use soap, remember God's Word.

O God, thank You for providing Your great Word, the Bible. Where would we be if it were not for this Book? Help me to read it, cherish it, understand it, and apply it in my life today. I pray in the name of Jesus. Amen.

China Isn't Just for Teacups!

The Toilet

Let no one say when he is tempted, "I am being tempted by God;" for God cannot be tempted by evil, and He Himself does not tempt anyone. But each one is tempted when he is carried away and enticed by his own lust. Then when lust has conceived, it gives birth to sin; and when sin is accomplished, it brings forth death. Do not be deceived, my beloved brethren ... Therefore putting aside all filthiness and all that remains of wickedness, in humility receive the word implanted, which is able to save your souls.

—James 1:13–16, 21

After years of cleaning toilets, my *most hated* household task, how could they have forgotten to send me a questionnaire? They just released a new National Study on Toilet Bowls, and I was not asked to participate! How could it be? I'll bet there are millions of other women out there who feel just the same as I do: slighted.

I realize this information will not be included in the National Study, but I want my toilet bowls on record. I have two: one white and one gray. Both are serviceable, both are cleaned regularly. Now, I feel better!

Every family must have at least one story about the bathroom bowl on file. Ours has several, but one favorite. When our son was almost two years old, he was beginning to be potty trained and loved the toilet. He would report that the toilet was "a-acky" and then "all done" often flushing it even when it was clearly only clean water going down. One day, my husband was home with a particularly bad case of the stomach flu. An "all done" was reported from the bathroom and the usual "whoosh" was heard. Proud mother. Proud father. Progress at last. The next time the bowl was flushed, it overflowed onto the nearly new carpet. What could be wrong? What could have plugged it? A little bit of investigating showed the bowl of decorator soap was empty. Guess who had flushed all nine pretty bars down the toilet? Having never experienced a plugged toilet before, we poured in both drain and toilet bowl cleaner. We had both studied chemistry but were too naïve to know these chemicals only fused all that soap together. It's a wonder the combined chemical fumes didn't exterminate our entire family! Finally, out of dire need, my husband unbolted the toilet from the floor and with the aid of a large (now discarded) butcher knife, removed nine colors of molded, fused soap from the neck of the bowl. While he removed that, I removed our son to another room for fear of bodily harm. His encouragement to his father by declaring the toilet "a-acky" was too overwhelming to a sick man.

While a toilet is a necessity in all homes, it is a constant reminder of filth and waste. As our bodies burn up food and create waste, so does sin in our lives burn up any desire to be fruitful for God. God does not place the temptation to sin before us, but we can be drawn away from Him by desiring to sin. Then when we sin, if we have not accepted Christ, we will die in that sin.

Just as a toilet is filled with filthiness and at times even overflows, spreading its filthiness further, a life full of sin can be pictured the same way. Have you accepted Christ's gift of pardon for your sin? If not, accept this gift, Jesus Christ, today. Be made clean and pure. If you already know Him, begin overflowing with good fruits, pleasing to God. This may not be a national survey, but God's records are the most important ones into which you will ever be included. Answer His "survey" today!

O Heavenly Father, thank You for this reminder in my home of the filthiness of my sin and how You have made me clean and pure by Christ's blood. Please forgive all my sin that stands between You and me. Please remove it from me. Thank you, dear Father. I pray in Jesus' name. Amen.

Knuckle Cracking

Chapped Hands

Behold, I have inscribed you on the palms of My hands; your walls are continually before Me.

—Isaiah 49:16

Want to become a millionaire and a benefactor of women around the globe? Just invent a cure for chapped hands and a way to prevent them. The masses of the female kingdom will bow down and pay homage to you!

My hands don't ever look like those models' hands in the magazines. (Where do they find these people, anyway?) I have these tiny, flat, wimpy nails that break all the time and knuckles that only a monkey could envy. The veins in the back of my hand are so large, the children used to use them for entertainment during sermons. *Will Mom's hand turn blue if I press on this big, fat vein and if I let go, will her hand turn pink again?* I always loved my mother's hands until I noticed them coming out of my sleeve. How can a person my age have such old-looking hands?

Try closing your eyes. Now visualize the shape of your hands, your fingernails, and your skin texture—don't try to kid yourself; that age spot is really there—your lifeline, and all the other little wrinkles your hands have. We have memorized how our hands look because we watch them working so many hours of every day.

In the same manner, God has memorized us because He has engraved us on the palms of His hands. He has not just engraved our names, but He has engraved *us*. He has memorized our personality, our character, and every minute detail about us. And, He says our ways are continuously before Him. He is constantly watching and watching out for us.

What a reassurance this verse is. God has me engraved in the palm of His hand. Every time I watch my hands dust, do dishes, or sweep this day, I will visualize myself engraved in God's palm and feel assurance. Keep your eye on those hands of yours, too.

Dear Heavenly Father, I thank You for this reminder of how much You care about me. You have my very image in front of You all the time. Remind me all day of that care. Because of this, give me Your peace, Your confidence. As I watch my hands today, may I remember Your hand, Your strength, Your love, Your caring. I ask all of this in the name of Jesus Christ. Amen.

My Bathroom Journal

"I promise to work on this room and not take on the organization of any other room until this bathroom is organized with safety, and refreshment."

1. Circle or name three major problem areas in your bathroom(s), prioritizing them with numbers.

    - Under-sink area cluttered
    - Not enough drawer storage (hair dryers, razors, towels, etc.)
    - Medication storage unsafe or limited
    - Need hooks to store clothing changes
    - Need more towel bars or shower storage for soaps, gels, etc.
    - Other:

    ____

    ____

2. Because I know God wants me to be clean and fresh every day, I am praying the following prayer for His customized solution:

    ____

    ____

    ____

3. The Scripture that has encouraged me to organize this bathroom is the following:

    ____

    ____

4. In order to complete my prioritized tasks, the supplies that I will need are the following:

   - Three containers for Trash, Donate, Save
   -
   -
   -
   -

(*This is a good time to read and follow along with "It's Time to Organize That Bathroom."*)

5. (*To be completed after your bathroom organizing job is finished.*)
   I see that God helped me accomplish organizing this bathroom. My feelings about this room are now (include today's date):

6. My *one year later* journal entry about this vital room is (include the date):

It's Time to Organize That

Bathroom

Did you think it was possible to actually study God's Word and find anything about a toilet, sink, towels, and hampers? Isn't it amazing how God is concerned and relevant to even this very necessary room and the tasks ahead? Throw the towels into the washer, and let's get started.

Let's do our "Circle Organizing" again. Start at the shower. Since bathrooms are usually small, the clutter problems would primarily be the following:

- Clothing dropped on floors
- Lack of cupboard storage for towels
- Lack of proper storage for medications

Those three containers are still needed: Trash, Donate, Save.

Shower

Can you reach and easily use shampoos and soaps? If needed, buy a new hanging or wall (pump-type) or corner-type holder for bottles. Stand in the shower and test the convenience of your new holders. Do you have several bottles of shampoos in the shower that you do not like? Clear them out, and start over with only what you actually use. Put up a high hook or two for wet washcloths to dry between uses if you reuse them.

Clothing Dropped on Floor

Inexpensive hooks can be purchased from any hardware

store to be installed on the back of the door, a wall behind the door, or any place *out of the way.* Store only daily robes or clothing that is removed in order to shower, and then clear the hooks off. Do not allow them to become just another cluttered area.

Storage for Towels

First, sort your towels, hand towels, and washcloths. Do you have ten bath towels and find you only use the favorite five all the time? Remove any unused towels or cloths and place in bins for storage and use later. Now that you have a more *reasonable quantity,* here is an area where you can become inventive. Using any empty wall space, you can install a small shelf to hold neatly stacked or rolled towels. A shelf can also be installed *above the doorway* allowing stacking/storage yet staying out of view from exterior rooms.

If possible, purchase a cabinet that goes above the toilet, and use this space to contain extra towels, toilet paper, and medications. If the sink cabinet will hold towels, place them here. Just keep them *contained,* neat, and out of sight.

Let's talk about *wet towels* and washcloths. Where do you store them now? Do you re-use bath/shower towels? If so, evaluate if you have enough towel bars or hooks to dry them properly. If you have a larger family, you may want to place some new hooks or bars on the walls or purchase over-the-door holders. If not overloaded, these can allow air to flow and towels to dry adequately without getting musty or moldy. There are several hangers that attach to door hinges or stand alone in the room. Care of wet towels can eliminate clutter, as well as mold and odors in the bathroom. Put a little money where your commitment is for an orderly bathroom.

Wet washcloths should be laid out to dry either in the bathroom or laundry area until time to launder them. Each family member should be instructed to do his or her part in the maintenance of the wet items in the bathroom. Only dried washcloths should be placed in the hamper. A separate bar or rack for this in the laundry area may solve the problem, especially if you have a larger family.

A Stress-Relieving Hint

May I share one of the best towel hints I ever received? When entertaining a large group of adults or children, clear off the counters and remove all the towels from your bathroom. Replace them with a roll of pretty paper towels on an attractive spindle. Many people sharing only one hand towel or using someone's bath towel is not only unappealing, it is unsanitary. This removes the pressure to have pretty, new hand or bath towels to display and actually makes the bathroom appear less cluttered. If you do this, don't forget to put an attractive waste basket nearby.

Medications

Begin with a *complete* sorting of all medications, purging anything that is even close to outdated. Also, evaluate any dangerous medications that could be reached by young children. These will need to be returned to the highest levels or put in some other safe place. The other medications should be grouped by uses and returned to the storage areas. These groups would be cold medications, first aid supplies, stomach medications, pain relievers, etc. If possible, use small baskets to contain your groups, labeling each one. This will also help in removing them when needed since so many medications come in small bottles or packages and may be stored above eye-level.

Health and beauty aids such as new supplies of shampoos, toothpaste, etc. can be stored with medications. Just remember to *group* supplies for easy access.

Bathroom Cleaning Supplies

You may want to keep a *limited, basic cleaning supply* under the sink or in an upper cabinet. A toilet bowl brush, toilet bowl cleaner, and sink cleaner would be easier accessed from under the sink each time the bathroom needs cleaning. *However,* if there are young children living or visiting in the home, consider their safety when storing harmful supplies.

A PERSONAL ORGANIZING STORY

Organizing any room is about meeting the needs of the family members who use that room. Not every client can be expected to be able to organize according to a plan. One such client had a personal need for all of his work shirts and pants to be within view and be in the bathroom instead of in his closet. Different, but that is what makes organizing a challenge. As I looked around the confined areas of the home and the bathroom, I asked the Lord to give me His eyes for an open space to meet the desires of this client yet keep it neat and uncluttered. As I closed the bathroom door and stepped inside alone, I found an open, inset area behind one bathroom door. That space allowed for two short clothing bars to be installed, enabling us to hang his clothing in that area. The clothing was out of sight when the door was opened, yet we were able to meet his need for *visual and tangible* access to his clothing in the bathroom. Granted, that area could have been very useful to hold extra towels and robes for the family, but his need was met, the bathroom remained orderly, and stressful mornings were avoided. God opened my eyes when I closed that bathroom door. He loves to keep it simple! Thanks, Lord!

Be sensitive to the needs of the family members who actually use those rooms, yet be creative to keep a sense of orderliness and cleanliness. New ways of doing things will not become habits if their needs are not considered. If it does not actually meet someone's needs, the organization will last only as long as you are willing to do all the daily maintenance of the area.

As you finish organizing the bathroom, throw out the trash, drive your donations to the collection center, and disperse the saved items wherever they belong.

Give Credit to the Lord

Dear Lord, I am thankful for the clean, orderly bathroom You have given me. I thank You for living in an age when we have such a luxury. Help me keep it in pleasant order so that my family and friends will be refreshed when they use it. Thank You for helping me. Amen.

Now go back a few pages and complete your *Bathroom Journal.*

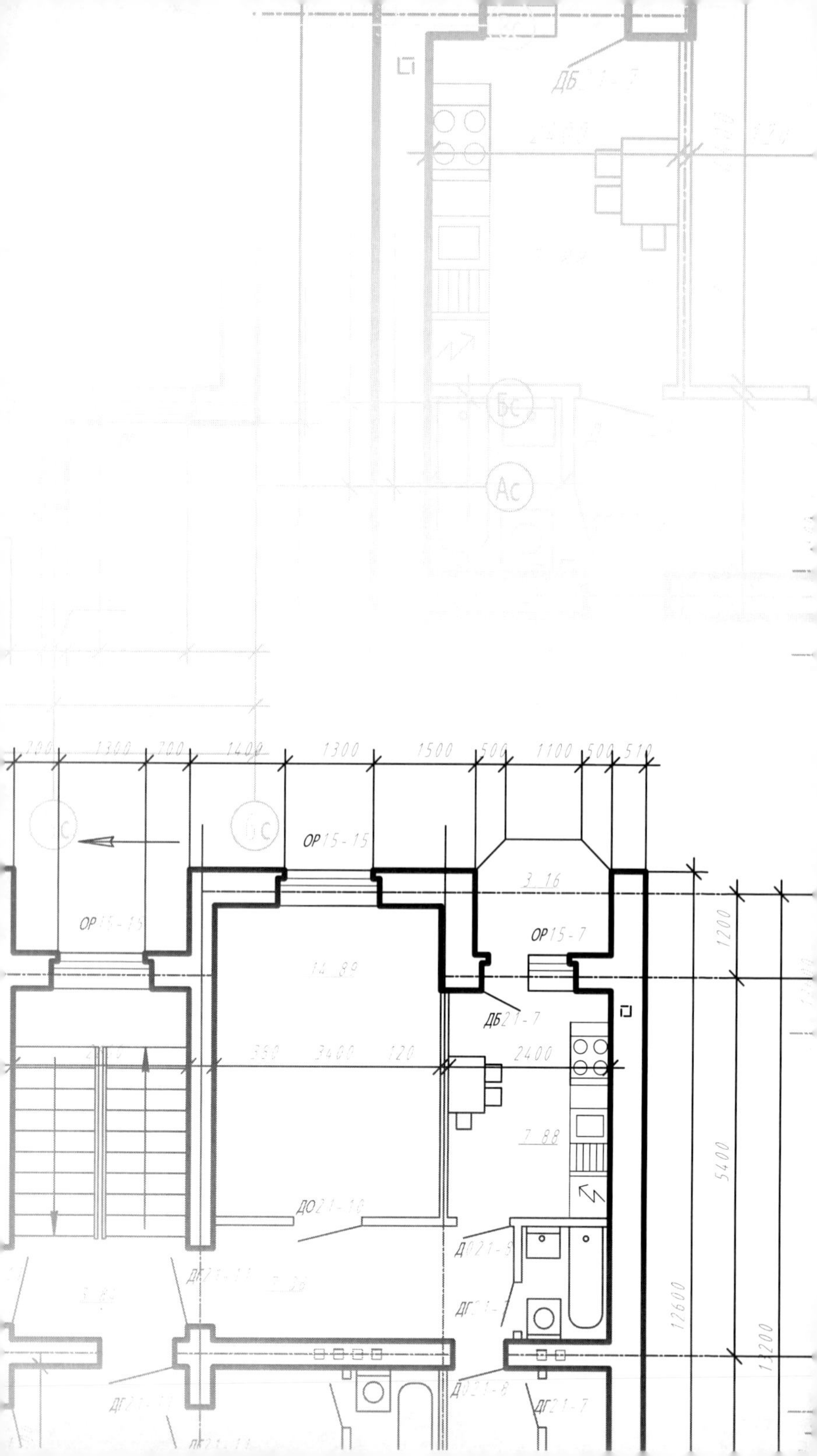
1300
700
1400
1300
1500
500
1100
500
510
ОР15-15
3.16
ОР15-7
1200
14.89
ДБ21-7
360
3400
120
2400
7.88
5400
ДО21-10
ДО21-9
ДГ21-7
12600
13200
ДО21-8
ДГ21-7

You Lint Up My Life

The Laundry Room

There is no glamour in doing laundry. Everyone has thought it drudgery since caveman days. We have the fastest, most efficient washers and dryers in history, yet we cannot get the clothing back into the drawers. What is wrong with us? Is it that we just don't care? I don't think so. Most likely, we need a better routine and some better "helps" in the laundry area. Let's look into God's Word, consider some "laundry stories" and pray over this necessary room in our home. With God's help, we can conquer our laundry problems … and I don't mean grease spots.

Precious Lord, I am moving on with Your help to clean and organize my laundry room. Will You help me put things in order here also? I want to have it organized so I can use my time more wisely. Help me decide how often to do laundry. By having this area organized, help me to finish the laundry each time I do it and not to have baskets and clothes sitting all over. Also, remind me that by caring for this room, I am respecting all the clothes and appliances You have given to me. I thank You for what I will be able to accomplish because of Your help. Amen.

On The Ropes

Clothespins

Therefore, since we have so great a cloud of witnesses surrounding us, let us also lay aside every encumbrance, and the sin which so easily entangles us, and let us run with endurance the race that is set before us.

—Hebrews 12:1

If you have ever lived in the country, perhaps you remember clothes hanging out on a clothesline to dry. I even recall my mother hanging clothes out to "freeze dry" in the middle of winter. Though it seems a little outdated now, I still love to hang my sheets and pillowcases on the line to dry and then enjoy the fresh, clean scent that only comes from crisp air, not a dryer.

I am so glad clothespins were invented in my lifetime. We have even managed to find some creative ways to use them like hooking the payment check to the newspaper box, clipping potato chip bags, or securing freshly glued popsicle-stick crafts. But when they are used for their intended purpose, they keep our fresh, clean wash tightly drawn to the line to crack in the breeze. How the pioneer women must have struggled without clothespins to hold their laundry fast to a line.

Life is like a clothespin many days. It seems bent on pinning us down firmly to an invisible line. We get so pinned down by everyday living that we cannot free ourselves to just worship or commune with God. How He wants us to set aside our daily routine and unburden ourselves so we can enjoy Him.

Also, have you ever noticed that when clothes do come loose from the line, it seems that they never come all the way off the clothesline? Instead, one corner always remains clipped tightly while the rest flaps in the dirt becoming dirtier with every stroke across the ground. So our lives seem to get caught in just one small area, and because of it, we get dirtier and dirtier. That one small area pins us to the world, and we seem to be twisted and thrown by every gust of wind.

Has your "clothespin" of a too-busy lifestyle gotten a tight grip on you? Or, are you held hostage by a habit you know would sadden the heart of God? Try living free from clothespins, the "pioneer laundry way."

Dear Father, I recognize that I have some areas and habits in my life that are not pleasing to You. I confess them and ask You for the strength to not keep repeating them. Help me to have freedom from them. I ask for Your help in Jesus' name. Amen.

Wrinkle Free

Fabric Softeners

And do not get drunk with wine, for that is dissipation, but be filled with the Spirit, speaking to one another in psalms and hymns and spiritual songs, singing and making melody with your heart to the Lord; always giving thanks for all things in the name of our Lord Jesus Christ to God, even the Father . . . that He might present to Himself the church in all her glory, having no spot or wrinkle or any such thing; but that she should be holy and blameless.

—Ephesians 5:18–20, 27

There are women who brag that they never have to iron. They won't iron! How do they do this? I must have my closets so tightly packed that almost everything comes out needing a touch-up ironing job. That is also true of some of the things in the drawers. This becomes especially true when I travel.

But this winter I discovered a new product that just sprays from the bottle, and the wrinkles disappear. Using it while doing laundry on vacation, a lady came up to me and asked to see it work. She told me she saw me spraying the wrinkles out and told her husband, "That lady's got something there!" I suddenly became the laundry demonstration guru for all the other laundromat customers who gathered around to see it work. And work it does! Wrinkles on clothing from the suitcase just wilted when I applied it. Wrinkles on hot clothing from the dryer fell out smooth enough to lie flat and straight. It is a miracle product.

Problems and sins in our lives can become like wrinkles on our clothing. They press together, messing up our appearance or reputation or peace of mind. They make us feel mashed down, confined, and messy. But then, when we choose to "spray" the Spirit of the Lord onto our lives, we feel His freedom releasing us to praise Him. As we confess all sin and thank Him, singing in our own spirit to Him, our lives begin to feel "straightened out." That new life we feel is holy to Him and to us.

Have you checked your wrinkles lately? Are you in need of the "new" miracle product? Decide to daily apply the Holy Spirit, and keep the ironing board in your life put away!

O dear Lord, I feel like wrinkled laundry today. I feel messed up; I feel out of control. Will You please forgive me of all my sin and renew the Holy Spirit in my life? I need to have You keep my life straightened out. I am unable to manage it myself. Please remind me this day as I touch any laundry that You have removed my "wrinkles" of sin and You have sprayed my life with the strength of the Holy Spirit to help me stay on track. Thank You, Lord Jesus. Amen.

ERMA AND LAUNDRY

Like everything in the house, Erma Bombeck wrestled with the washing machine and its consumption of socks.

> So men are planning a trip to the moon. So computers run every large industry in America. So body organs are being transplanted like perennials.
>
> Big deal! You show me a washer that will launder a pair of socks and return them to you as a pair, and I'll light a firecracker.
>
> I never had what you would call a good relationship with washers. They hate me. They either froth at the lid, walk across the utility room or just plain quit. But mostly they have a sock deficiency that defies reason.[4]

As The Dial Turns

Washing Machines

Who among you is wise and understanding? Let him show by his behavior his deeds in the gentleness of wisdom. But if you have bitter jealousy and selfish ambition in your heart, do not be arrogant and so lie against the truth. This wisdom is not that which comes down from above, but is earthly, natural, and demonic. For where jealousy and selfish ambition exist, there is disorder and every evil thing. But the wisdom from above is first pure, then peaceable, gentle, reasonable, full of mercy and good fruits, unwavering, without hypocrisy. And the seed whose fruit is righteousness is sown in peace by those who make peace.

—James 3:13–18

Our electric bill had passed the three-digit mark and was still climbing. I had to fight off the urge to smash the electric meter or unleash the dog on the meter man.

In an effort to reduce our electrical consumption, we purchased an old wringer washer and tubs at a garage sale. It didn't cost a lot to run one of those babies back when, so I figured I could cut that electric bill with just a little extra energy on my part. So now, instead of turning the dial and leaving, I pull the knob, turn the lever, lift the wet, heavy clothes through two rinses, run them through the wringers, and do extra ironing because of all the wrinkles. Did you know those two little rollers can suck a hand through them up to the wrist in less than three seconds? And did you know that skin exposed to cold tap water for a period of more than thirty minutes not only has the texture of a prune, but the color of one also? Amazing! Yes, I am really saving energy. I'm saving so much energy that, on wash day, I am completely exhausted!

A wringer washer, though being criticized here, accomplishes the very same task as an automatic washer. It saves electricity and water and is faster, but it is also far less convenient. In the end, both washers deliver the same product: clean clothes.

How like wringers and automatics are Christians! Many believers work long hours at leisurely paces perhaps wasting a little more paper or gasoline; while others work fast, furiously, and conservatively yet need much assistance and supervision. But somehow, all the work of Christ's church seems to get done.

It is so easy to praise one person's work over another or to be critical of someone who has a small, easy task or appears to not be working at all. In Christ's great plan, each is accomplishing some of His goals: to spread the Word, to be like Him, and to be obedient. While each Christian does it a different way, a Christ-follower cannot help but reveal Him in their life.

In your church, be careful not to criticize the wringers or automatics. The next time you load that washer, remember what God's Word said about envy, strife, bitterness, and hypocrisy.

Then, throw in a load of wisdom with a cup of purity. Now set your wash cycle to peacefulness, gentleness, and soften it all with mercy and good fruits. Every washer will turn out the same product... Christ-filled Christians.

Our dear Heavenly Father, I thank You today for my washer. Thank You for its reminder that all of Your followers are not working in the same way, but we are working toward the same goal. Help me to be unwilling to yield to the temptation of jealousy, pride, and self-centeredness. Please help me to add peacefulness, gentleness, and mercy to my life today. Help me to fill the world around me with Your peace. Amen.

Sauna Savings

The Dryer

Yet you do not know what your life will be like tomorrow. You are just a vapor that appears for a little while and then vanishes away.

—James 4:14

We were thinking "green" before it was even popular! Watching the steam form outdoors from my dryer vent, I felt guilt and thrift hit me at the same time. I talked my husband into installing one of those indoor/outdoor vents on the dryer.

After a simple procedure of pulling out the dryer, ripping apart the vent tube, and installing the new vent, we were ready to pump warm, moist air through our house instead of into the great outdoors. The laundry room is not large, but I rationalized that the heat would rise out into the kitchen and other rooms.

The first few loads proved I was right. That room was toasty warm. Of course, the window was steamed up and there was a trace of moisture on the paneling, but the room was warmer. After about five more loads, I decided there might be a few flaws in my plan. The steam had formed so much moisture on the paneling it was running down the wall. A small stream of water was also now running down the floor from the vent opening into the closet, and my son had written his name and several pictures on the steamy window. Having a half-bath in this same room, the toilet tank and seat were sweaty and—well, sticky. But my fern, ivy, and violets loved it!

I tried this great idea for only a few more loads over the next few weeks. Admitting defeat, I glued the loosened floor tiles, waxed the paneling, and removed the new vent. Who would think that a little steam could do all that?

Vapor is compared to our lives, and truly, I can see the comparison the older I get. It seems a few weeks ago I was a girl, yesterday a young mother (trying to save a few pennies with recycled steam), and today I am diapering my grandchildren. Oh, that the vapor could stand still instead of flowing onward.

My dryer's vapor left many effects: happy plants, loose tile, and peeling walls. What effect has your life or vapor left so far? With your next sighting of vapor or steam, remember to watch it vanish. Then, remember with God's help to do the best with that vapor every day as it flows from you onward and upward.

O dear God, I believe Psalms 90:12 when You told me to "number" my days so that I present to You a life that has been lived in wisdom and discernment. I appreciate this day You have given me and commit it to You. Help my "vapor" saturate lives for Your glory. I pray in Jesus' name. Amen.

"Do not remove a fly from your friend's forehead with a hatchet."[5]

Chinese Proverb

Quiet Needling

The Sewing Machine

For we hear that some among you are leading an undisciplined life, doing no work at all, but acting like busybodies. Now such persons we command and exhort in the Lord Jesus Christ to work in quiet fashion and eat their own bread.

—II Thessalonians 3:11–12

Perhaps you do not like to sew or do not own or want a sewing machine, but I formed an attachment to mine many years ago. Is there a machine in my home that can match this miracle worker?

I remember purchasing this little gem several years ago. A trip downtown with a one-year-old and a three-year-old to look at sewing machines bordered on insanity, but I was never one for having my feet on the ground anyway. I thought, *I can make this little baby pay for itself in mending alone.* And it did. Those first few years of use saw blue jeans, T-shirts, bibs, dresses, dress shirts, table cloths, and bushels of other things renovated to last months longer. Later, I graduated it to sewing skirts, trousers, suits, and even upholstering. Today, I treasure that little machine right next to hot running water and electricity.

I have heard other sewing machines rattle and clunk or just buzz. But in all those years, I always noticed its quiet motor. *Hum, hum, hum.* It was never noisy, just running along, quietly stitching one stitch at a time, smoothly and evenly.

How much Christ wants us to be like my old, reliable sewing machine. No clatter, no disarray, no buzzing. But instead, He wants quiet, steady workers who can later enjoy the fruit of their labor. Notice He wants quiet, but not silent, workers.

How do we get to be quiet workers? By meditating on the Word each day, taking it in our hearts to our work and there, because of the peace the Holy Spirit gives us, we begin to work quietly yet ever so effectively. How is your "sewing machine" running? Got a clink here and a plunk there? Oil it up daily with the Word, and begin humming quietly.

Dear Father, I want to be a quiet worker for You today. Forgive my attitude of wanting to bring attention to myself by gossiping and criticizing others. Quiet my spirit today as I focus on Your Word. Help me to "work in a quiet fashion" this day, for I desire to honor You with the work I do. Amen.

Odor Incubator

The Hamper

I ask on their behalf; I do not ask on behalf of the world, but of those whom Thou has given Me; for they are Thine ... I have given them Thy word; and the world has hated them, because they are not of the world, even as I am not of the world. I do not ask Thee to take them out of the world, but to keep them from the evil one. They are not of the world, even as I am not of the world. Sanctify them in the truth; Thy word is truth. As Thou didst send Me into the world, I also have sent them into the world. And for their sakes I sanctify Myself, that they themselves also may be sanctified in the truth.

—John 17:9, 14–19

There are really only two disgustingly smelly fixtures in every household. At the top of the list is a bathroom fixture, and running a close second, is the hamper. Perhaps the word "disgusting" is a bit mild for the hamper.

Not everyone has the pleasure of living on a farm, but we did. My experience taught me that pants cuffs always are a hazard to the farmwife. She learns never to remove jeans by the cuffs or she may find herself smelling like the barn floor. The athlete's mother opens the hamper to the pungent odor of sweaty sneaker socks and a stiff, perspiration-filled uniform. The mechanic's wife sometimes finds that her lingerie in the hamper smells like yesterday's oil change, and a few new black dots have been added to her white silk blouse. A proud, young, new mother faces reality when she opens her hamper, and it smells like pureed spinach, over-ripe bananas, and sour formula. And what woman has not been proud to find that her husband finally picked up his towel from the bathroom floor only to throw it, soaking wet, into the hamper where it mildewed her white tablecloth? Hampers have been given a bad name, and they deserve it!

How much like a hamper is the world and mankind like the clothing thrown into it. Some people wallow in sin, getting themselves filthy and enjoying it. They absorb all they can get in the name of fun or thrills. Some people just get a few spots of sin here and there in their lives. Some people have no sin we can see; they are "good" people, yet they smell or repulse God because they have not become a believer in Christ. Then there is the Christian. Because of Christ, he is made of absolutely soil-resistant fabric. To God, the Christian is spotless, sweet-smelling because he is completely covered by Christ.

But Christ does not desire to have us removed from this hamper of foul, dirty clothes—the world. He says He has given us God's Word to sanctify (or purify) believers and intercedes for them constantly to the Father "to keep them from the evil one."

Open your hamper and take a good look and a good whiff. Begin thanking God that He has placed you in this "hamper" called life. Now realize that because of Christ's great love, you are sweet-smelling, and that Christ Himself is interceding for you constantly in order to keep you that way. Happy hampering!

Dear Father, I know the "hamper" You have put me in is designed just for me. You want me here, and You will keep me. I trust that today. Wash me and make me clean again and keep me from soiling my life, my testimony for You. Amen.

The Original Black Holes in Space

Pockets

But just as it is written, "Things which eye has not seen and ear has not heard, and which have not entered the heart of man, all that God has prepared for those who love Him." For to us God revealed them through the Spirit; for the Spirit searches all things, even the depths of God. For who among men knows the thoughts of a man except the spirit of the man, which is in him: Even so the thoughts of God no one knows except the Spirit of God.

—I Corinthians 2:9–11

A hand would have no home if it were not for pockets. Every garment worth owning has at least one pocket. What would life be like if pockets were eliminated from carpenters' aprons, purses, skirts, blue jeans, jackets, shirts, and housewives' aprons? Not only would there be a lot of homeless hands, but half the designer labels in America would be eliminated.

Pockets at our house need to be the size of an average tote bag. Car keys? In the pocket. Coins? In the pocket. Hairbrushes? In the pocket. Tissues, pens, pencils, calculators, checkbooks, cookies, apples, nails, screwdrivers, socks (clean and dirty) have all been found in pockets at our house. Searching these pockets on laundry day is a job that should offer hazardous duty pay. Barn coveralls always offer a special challenge. Many ears of corn, huge tractor bolts, and jars of animal medicine have come from those pockets. From the teenagers' blue jeans come love notes, car keys, padlocks, half-eaten candy, and homework that was never turned in to the teacher. From the ten-year-old boys' pockets tumble toy cars, marbles, string, a rubber spider, a fishing lure, and bubble gum, already chewed. From the girls' pockets come a hand mirror, strawberry lip-gloss, mascara, nail polish, one rainbow shoelace, and a picture of a movie star with lip prints on it. Searching a person's pockets can give a pretty accurate picture of what is important in the owner's life.

The Holy Spirit searches the deep thoughts and desires of God, just as we search deep pockets to find hidden treasures. That same Holy Spirit reveals these deep treasures to us. We could never search for and find these treasures from men. These are God's treasures, God's words, God's teachings for our lives.

Have you searched any good pockets today? As you do, desire the Holy Spirit to search out the deep things of God to reveal to you this day. Happy treasure hunting!

As I search empty pockets today, Lord, I am thinking how You have left me the Holy Spirit to search Your deepest thoughts about me. Please reveal those to me in the quietness of my heart. Speak to me, Holy Spirit. I want to understand my Father more. Help me to understand His love for me that was so great that He would sacrifice His only Son for me. O God, this is too deep for me to understand, but I feel Your love just from having this knowledge. Thank You, dear God. In the name of Christ I pray. Amen.

My Laundry Journal

"I promise to work on this room and not take on the organization of any other room until this laundry room and my laundry habits are in proper order."

1. Circle or name three major problem areas in your laundry room or routine, prioritizing them with numbers.

   - Laundry room too small, cluttered
   - Laundry room too large, no limits, cluttered
   - Room has too many uses (examples: entry, coats, games, toys, etc.)
   - No cupboard or shelf space for cleaning products
   - Too many cleaning products or unrelated products
   - Laundry seldom folded and put away on laundry day
   - Baskets of laundry located around house
   - Other:

   ____

   ____

2. Because I know God provides clothing for us and wants me to enjoy caring for it, my prayer for God's customized solution to my laundry area and habits is:

   ____

   ____

   ____

3. The Scripture that has encouraged me to organize my laundry area and habits is the following:

____

____

____

4. In order to complete my prioritized tasks, the supplies that I will need are the following:

- Three Containers for Trash, Donate, Save
-
-
-
-

(This is a good time to read and follow along with "It's Time to Organize That Laundry Room.")

5. (*To be completed after organization of laundry area and trying new habits for no less than 2 weeks.*)
   I see that God has helped me accomplish organizing this project. My feelings about my laundry and habits are now (include today's date):

____

____

____

____

6. My *one year later* journal entry about my laundry room and habits is (include the date):

It's Time to Organize That

Laundry Room

The biggest problem that I observe in organizing laundry areas is not always so much the physical space, but the laundry habits. But we need to *start with the area* before we organize your habits. Let's walk through the process together, and it will help you define your needs.

Whether you have a laundry area in a closet or an entire room dedicated to it, the organizing will be very similar. We will take each possibility separately.

Again, get those three containers: Trash, Donate, Save.

Small Laundry Area in a Closet

Mobile homes and even some homes have only allowed for a laundry area the size of a closet. In this case, making the best use of the small space is particularly necessary.

Begin by sorting all detergents and laundry items. If you have only a shelf above your washer and dryer, *think about replacing it with a cabinet with doors.* Place all laundry soaps, bleaches, and softening materials in this area.

Perhaps you will choose to store extra or dangerous cleaning materials in this cupboard. This would make a good choice since it would be high and very hard for young children to reach.

Install a small rod or large hook to hold hangers on which to place clothing as it comes out of the dryer.

Store empty laundry baskets *on top* of the cupboard.

Install small, stick-up hooks on the wall or a retractable line to hold lingerie that must be air dried. A small trash bag can also be hung here to collect dryer lint.

Be sure to have doors installed (if they do not exist) on the closet area to close off the laundry from view. If you are unable to use doors, use attractive curtains or a large window blind. Concealment is the goal.

Full-Sized Laundry Room

So many homes are built with the laundry area at the back door (mud room idea) or it is located in the basement and is not really enclosed as a room so things just flow together even though they are not related to laundry. Our intention must be to make a *designated laundry area* and organize the rest of the room or area.

Washer, Dryer, and Cleaning Products

See the article above for the "small laundry area in closet." Please realize that the laundry area only needs the same space even in a larger room.

Evaluate the shelf or cabinet above the washer and dryer. An enclosed cabinet is recommended, and if your room is large enough, a pantry-type cabinet next to the washer or dryer will give additional storage for those cleaning products. Try your best to keep it all behind doors, not on a shelf and not visible. Begin by sorting all detergents and laundry items, and place them in one area. Perhaps you will choose to store extra or dangerous cleaning materials in this cupboard. This would make a good choice since it would be high and very hard for young children to reach.

Install a small rod or large hook to hold hangers on which to place clothing as it comes out of the dryer. With this much space, you can put up a table to be used for folding laundry. Also, keep your iron and ironing board standing, ready to use. Or install one of the wall units that keep the iron and board from view yet are easily accessed. Just remember that these two surfaces cannot become storage areas for anything. They are for laundry and ironing only and need to be cleared each time laundry is done.

Store empty laundry baskets *on top* of the cupboard. Just because you have extra floor space, think about *compacting* the area. Also, you may be able to hang the baskets on a large hook, keeping them up and out of the way.

Install small stick-up hooks or a retractable line to hold delicates that must be air dried. A small trash bag can also be hung or a waste basket needs to be nearby to collect dryer lint.

If you have a sink, you could add a small shelf and/or cabinet above it to use that wall space as well. This should be enough to make an actual laundry area useable. Make decisions about the use of the rest of the room.

Mud Room/Entry

If there is no coat closet in your entry area, building or creating one will need to be a priority. Coats and seasonal coverings need to be stored and out of sight. If you are fortunate enough to be able to afford to have cubicles built, by all means, do this. Or visit your local furniture store and purchase locker or divided units for each individual. There are so many do-it-yourself models available that can add character and organization to your entry. These can provide extra space for shoes, boots, jackets, etc. If drawers are not available, a pretty basket on top of the cubicles for each person can hold mittens, scarves, hats, etc. and even add color/character to the room. For those who prefer that everyone remove their shoes before entering carpeted areas, provide a shoe storage cubicle or shoe shelves of some sort to keep the entry clear. If your kids can do it at Mickey D's, everyone should be able to do it at home! Just remember to keep all storage simple with clean lines.

These are additional helps you might add:

- A set of hooks for keys
- A bulletin board or dry erase board for chores, pictures, reminders, etc.
- A small table or cabinet to hold items that must go out or come in for each family member (purses, briefcase, schoolbooks, gifts on occasion, etc.)

If your budget or space will not allow for all your clothing in either the lockers or a closet, sort by season, and store extras (sealed and labeled) in another area. Bring out only what can be used for a particular season.

Remember, this is a point of entry to your home that just happens to also serve as a laundry area. Concealing your washer, dryer, and all related items will bring a sense of order to this important room. The task is to make it pleasant to look at, be serviceable for laundry, and still serve the needs of your family.

Basement Laundry Room

This type of laundry room has the same problem organizing as the two types already discussed. Complete all the tasks already mentioned for the "Laundry/Mud Room."

Now, notice if your area has spread out too far in the basement. Create "walls" *enclosing your space,* by using folding dividers, tall furniture around your area, curtains or sheets, or use an area rug to define the dimensions. *A designated area is the goal.*

The main idea here is to *stop the spread.* Determine the limits of your area, and be creative at enclosing your laundry space. This will make it more pleasing to the eye and help you keep it organized in the future.

Set definite limits about what can be stored or used in your laundry area. Pay attention to shelves. Be firm on this with other family members as well as yourself.

Organize Your Laundry Routine and Habits

Understand, this may take a few trials to see what works best for you, but here are some basic organizational ideas that apply:

- Washing every day leaves laundry never finished.
- Unfolded laundry takes more work to make it look good than folding directly from the dryer.
- Laundry sitting around in baskets makes the home messy looking and no one can find their clothing quickly which wastes time.

Only your determination to complete the process of washing, folding, and returning all clothing to closets and drawers can make any process a success.

These are some organizational suggestions for your routine:

Try washing one or two times a week.

Depending on your family size, this may work for you. Try washing clothing and towels on one regular wash day. Then, about three days later, wash sheets and towels only. This will allow for the folding and putting away processes to be *completed* on the wash day. No baskets will be sitting around, and no hampers will be overflowing with wet towels.

Take note that to begin this routine will require an evaluation on your part to see if each family member has about eight pairs of underwear, eight pairs of socks, eight shirts, three pairs of pants or jeans, etc. You get the idea!

Try washing every other day if you have always washed every day.

Whatever schedule you decide to try, the real success will come from your determination to wash, fold, and *put away* the laundry the same day you do it. Trial and error will be your best guides to a schedule that works for you. But do try to break the old habits that you have had if laundry organization has been a problem for you.

Make laundry a family task.

Many children still grow up not knowing dryer lint from a dust bunny. You can instill many good habits like responsibility, cooperation, thriftiness, and neatness by incorporating your family's help with the laundry. Just as we would not turn our graduating child loose with a car and a credit card without proper training, why do we think we can do that with their clothing? Teens will probably resist this, but they will thank you when they get to the dorm or get married. Smaller children will begin to accept this as just part of the weekly routine. Even the youngest children can become part of the program. And don't forget, Dad can set the example, too.

A PERSONAL ORGANIZING STORY

One young client had a really difficult time getting laundry done, much less putting it away in the drawers and closets. Teaching two preschoolers to help her sort and return laundry to dressers seemed impossible. Asking the Lord for a creative, child-friendly solution, I looked around their rooms for what they already had to use for guides. Several magazines, catalogs, crayons and markers were on their desk. The answer came in one word, "pictures." I suggested that we label the children's drawers with pictures of the clothing items and label the shelves in the closet with pictures of shoes and games. We carefully printed the name of the item so that along with learning where to put their clothes, they could learn to read the words. When I returned for the next visit, not only were the children putting their clothes away, but her husband was helping more as well because he now could remember where the children's clothes were stored. She relieved herself from a lot of stress, the house looked less messy, the children were learning to take responsibility for helping and learning to take better care of their clothing. As a bonus, her husband felt good about being part of this new process that helped his wife. She found that some simple pictures and a few minutes of instruction with the family made a difference in her life, the home, and the family's cooperation in running a "smooth ship." Just like Jesus used the items He had at hand, we can do that too. We just need a little prayerful direction to see what to use. Customized catalogs, crayons and markers!

You are in control of your laundry destiny. Like any good administrator, be firm, be creative, be innovative, and delegate, delegate, delegate.

Before you close the laundry room door, empty the trash, send donations out, and disperse the saved items to rooms and family members.

Give Credit to the Lord.

Now that you have organized your laundry area and routines, take time to thank the Lord for His personal direction in accomplishing this.

Lord, You know that laundry is not a fun job and that I do it because I love my family. Please help me to keep it done, folded, and put away. Give me the strength to be flexible in trying to form new habits and routines. I know You have helped me with the enormous task of rearranging this laundry area. I appreciate all the clothing You have given to me and to my entire family. Please help me use even this room as a testimony of Your help to me. Today I pray about each family member as I care for their clothing, thanking You for them and asking You to meet their needs today. I thank You again. Amen.

Now go back a few pages and complete your *Laundry Journal.*

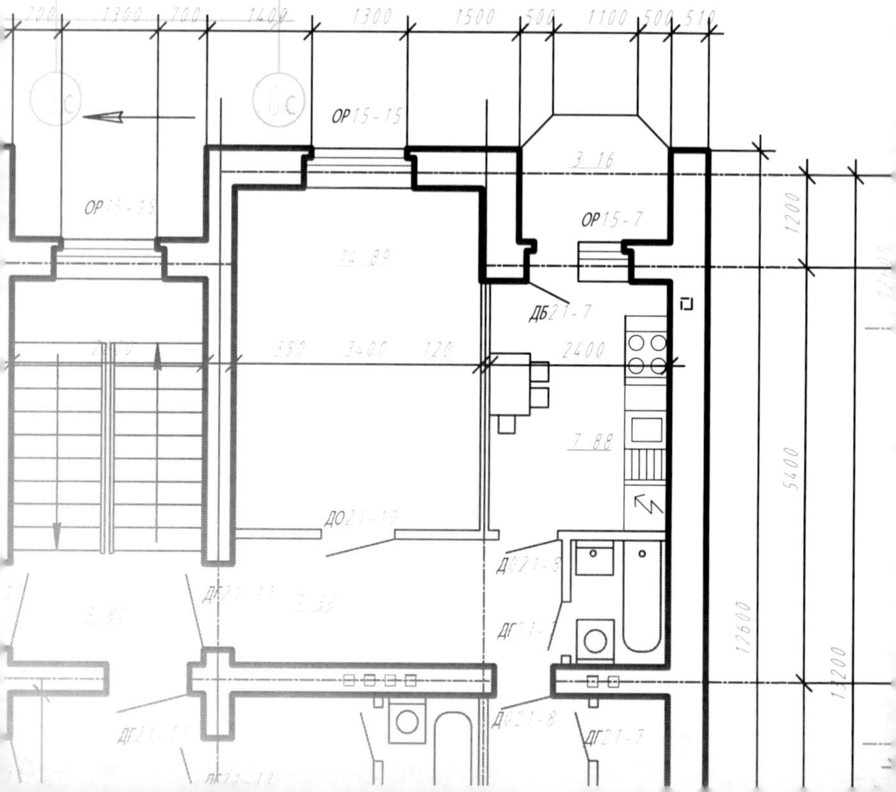
700
1300
700
1400
1300
1500
500
1100
500
510
ОР15-15
ОР15-7
14.89
ДБ21-7
3.16
2400
7.88
3400
120
ДО21-8
ДГ21-7
1200
5400
12600
13200

Tools on Board, but I'm Jumping Ship

Cleaning Supplies/Closet

It is no wonder that we don't always keep a clean house... we cannot always find our cleaning tools. They get scattered all over the house with little rhyme or reason where we leave them. We need to have a *centralized area* and a *plan* for cleaning in order to do a good job. And we want to do a good job. We know that having a clean house promotes good health for our family, it protects and preserves our furnishings, and it gives us a sense of accomplishment.

Now, let's take time to think about how God can be reflected in a clean home. Take time to pray over your cleaning habits and ask God to give you a plan to use your time and tools wisely.

Dear Lord, You know that I want to keep this home clean and orderly. Help me today to learn where to store these cleaning items so I can do an efficient job. Please help me to not waste time or energy yet keep a home that is pleasant for all to enter. I want to use this clean house for You. I am praying for this in Jesus' name. Amen.

Scrub Brush versus Mop

Floor Care

As each one has received a special gift, employ it in serving one another, as good stewards of the manifold grace of God. Whoever speaks, let him speak, as it were, the utterances of God; whoever serves, let him do so by the strength which God supplies; so that in all things God may be glorified through Jesus Christ, to whom belongs the glory and dominion forever and ever. Amen.

—I Peter 4:10–11

The Dutch have a reputation for cleanliness. To be raised by a Dutch mother, one would learn that cleanliness started at the bottom of a room and went upward. My Dutch mother taught me this and, therefore, would never even allow a mop into our home. It was the scrub brush. No, not a scrub brush on a handle but a scrub brush used by hand while on your knees with close scrutiny to every crack, crevice, and corner of the floor.

A person was not only required to use a scrub brush on hands and knees, but was never permitted to use anything but a bar of soap to get the desired results. A separate bucket for scrubbing and rinsing and several water changes soon produced a glistening, clean floor. (Are you getting a vision of Cinderella here?) Our wax never yellowed because it was always removed between applications. Our floors were literally clean enough to eat off them!

Today, I am so glad my mother taught me how to really get a floor clean. Though I do now own a mop, I only use it to clean up between thorough scrubbings. Mom gave me the ability to work hard, achieve cleanliness, and appreciate the results. So many people have been deprived of proper training in many areas of their lives and, therefore, lack the abilities to do certain things.

Think back about the training you have received. Do you appreciate and use the abilities you already have? Recognize that your ability is given to you from God. He gave you some inner ability, a gift to be used. Next, commit that ability and its use to Him.

. . . that in all things God may be glorified through Jesus Christ, to whom belongs the glory and dominion forever and ever. Amen.

—I Peter 4:11b

Can you imagine how effective our churches would be if we all would recognize our abilities and then apply them in a ministry? I am so thankful for the health to scrub, the training of how to do an immaculate job, and for a Savior to Whom I can commit this job for His glory. What abilities do you have to consider today?

O precious Father, thank You for the ability You have given me to keep a clean house. Thank You for the training I had in my childhood. Help me today to recognize that all my abilities come from You and that each one is designed to aid Your great plan for my life. I ask that You bless the work of my hands and body today that You may be glorified. Amen.

"Thar She Blows ..."
Vacuum Cleaner

There is no one holy like the Lord, indeed there is no one besides Thee, nor is there any rock like our God.

—I Samuel 2:2

And behold, there arose a great storm in the sea, so that the boat was covered with the waves; but He Himself was asleep. And they came to Him and awoke Him saying, "Save us, Lord; we are perishing!" And He said to them, "Why are you timid, you men of little faith?" Then He arose and rebuked the winds and the sea; and it became perfectly calm.

—Matthew 8:24–27

A twenty-year-old vacuum cleaner would be considered an antique by some, but I consider it my right-hand man! Almost daily I follow this scuffed-up brown bag of wind around the house pushing it through my worst messes. This old vacuum has cleaned more carpet, more walls, more furniture, and more cars than I care to count.

Dependable as it is, there are a few things that it dislikes picking up. One is sand. The area near the back door seems to be constantly gritty with sand. By lowering the vacuum head, the sand is easily cleaned up. But if the clean-out zipper is left open on the vacuum bag, the sand is just as quickly deposited on my jeans and in my shoes. Entering a boys' bedroom, we find the vacuum begins to make *plunk, clunk, ping,* and tumble noises. When it is turned off, we find it spits out an array of BBs, marbles, nuts, bolts, springs, and one pet rock. It refuses to beat out and retrieve any heavy, solid matter!

For Christians, the world around us is like a giant

vacuum. It is constantly trying to beat us down, blow us over, or take us into its grasp. If we are depending on Christ, we can be like those BBs, marbles, or rocks; we don't move. We are weighted, anchored, attached to Christ. Nothing can move us or harm us when our lives are built upon Him.

Do you have loved ones or friends who have never believed in Jesus' gift of Himself for them? Their lives are only built upon themselves, their own strengths and abilities. Like sand, they will be defeated, sucked up and blown away by the storms of life. They have nothing solid or sure to build on, lean on, or depend upon.

With every push of your vacuum, thank God for the illustrations of wind, sand, and rocks. Thank Him for providing another type of rock in your life, "The Rock," the precious Lord Jesus Christ.

Dear precious Lord, thank You for being the Rock in my life. Thank You for loving me, for holding onto me even when I let go of You. You see the storms in my life, and I praise You today for the assurance that it will not overtake me because You are holding onto me. Amen.

Whisk It Away

Broom and Dustpan

Trust in the Lord with all your heart, and do not lean on your own understanding. In all your ways acknowledge Him, and He will make your paths straight.

—Proverbs 3:5–6

A broom has to be one of the finest inventions of man. Few household tools are as versatile as a broom. Cover it with an old T-shirt and you can sweep down the highest cobwebs. Is something caught in the vacuum cleaner hose? Ram a broom handle down it to push it out the other end. Brooms also make the best dog chasers, snow sweepers for the front porch, and spider killers in the garage. Brooms can be used on linoleum, tile, concrete, and even carpeting.

As wonderful as the broom is, I have yet to find a dustpan to equal it. No matter how hard I try, I always end up with dirt under or beside my dustpan. If I push a large pile of dirt, it spreads out over the dustpan, falling beside and behind it. If I push too gently, I leave a fine layer of dirt, and the dustpan rolls right over it. The most skilled housewife cannot direct dirt into that dustpan in one stroke.

In regular sweeping, have you ever noticed the many ways you push a broom? Short taps clean the corners; long sweeps drag the dirt together into the center of the room. Bend over to pick up a safety pin off the floor, and you find you will automatically lean against the broom. All sweeping is done pressing our weight, pushing our strength, leaning into the broom.

Trusting the Lord in our daily lives takes a lot of "leaning." We cannot lean on our families, our friends, our church, or even our own talents and strength to see us through each day. We must lean on Christ. Just like a good firm broom, we can lean on Him to remove cobwebs from our lazy brains, to chase away the evil one from our presence, and to unclog frustrating problems in our lives. He desires to sweep sin out of our nature, daily. Like a perfect broom, we can depend on Him to give us direction in what we do, in what we say, and how we live.

As you sweep your floor today, acknowledge Him as the support in your life. Lean on that broom; have a holy life directed and swept up with holy living to please Him.

O dear God, my life needs a lot of sweeping out and cleaning up. Please show me corners I need to clean out and cobwebs that I need to bring down. I trust You to help me to make my life blameless. I cannot do it quickly, I know, in one big sweep. But help me to make areas of my life holy. I give those to You. I am leaning on You. Amen.

"The secret of my success? It is simple. It is found in the Bible, 'In all thy ways acknowledge Him and He shall direct thy paths.'"

George Washington Carver

The Richness of Rags

Dusting

Now the birth of Jesus Christ was as follows. When His mother Mary had been betrothed to Joseph, before they came together she was found to be with child by the Holy Spirit. And Joseph her husband, being a righteous man, and not wanting to disgrace her, desired to put her away secretly. But when he had considered this, behold, an angel of the Lord appeared to him in a dream, saying "Joseph, son of David, do not be afraid to take Mary as your wife for that which has been conceived in her is of the Holy Spirit. And she will bear a Son; and you shall call His name Jesus, for it is He who will save His people from their sins." Now all this took place that what was spoken by the Lord through the prophet might be fulfilled, saying, "Behold, the virgin shall be with child, and shall bear a Son, and they shall call His name Immanuel," which translated means, "God with us." And Joseph arose from his sleep, and did as the angel of the Lord commanded him and took her as his wife, and kept her a virgin until she gave birth to a Son; and he called His name Jesus.

—Matthew 1:18–25

Call it the unseen job of any household: dusting. Who notices when surfaces are slicked clean? It is easy to notice a bunch of junk in the room, papers lying around, or dirty dishes all over the kitchen. But who notices if the chair rungs or the blades on the ceiling fan are dusty? Or who sees the inside of the entertainment cabinet where static electricity has caused a layer of dust an inch thick? No one—that's who notices dust.

And what do I use to do this unseen, insignificant job? Do I buy one of those bright new dusters? No, instead I make rags from old soft clothing. I cut them in about one-foot squares, a good size for my hand. After using them several times, I either wash them and reuse them or just throw them out in the trash. These old rags seem very insignificant, but just think what a house would look like or become if we never removed the dust from the surfaces. It could become a virtual health hazard to live in a dust-filled home!

Joseph would seem to be an unseen, insignificant part of Christ's life. But just think of his significance to Christ's life and to Mary's well-being. He saved Mary from shame and even stoning, made a home for her and Jesus, moving them to safety when God spoke to him. He raised Jesus to visit the Temple yearly, to study under Jewish scholars. He must have provided food, shelter, money, clothing—everything for the Messiah, yet he is not highly exalted in God's Word. He kept Mary a virgin until Christ was born. He listened to God with immediate obedience in each instance. He was willing to make personal sacrifices for God's plan. Perhaps he had a dream, like many of us do, to make great use of his skills yet left everything he knew and moved in order to save Mary and Jesus.

Do you feel insignificant? Do you feel your service for Christ is small? Is your corner of the world He has called you to serve in just "little"? How can we ever insult our mighty God by thinking where He has placed us is not of great importance to His plan? No job is insignificant to God, and no "tool," no servant is insignificant either. Remember Joseph as you remove the dust from your home today, and let your surface shine for Him.

Dear God, forgive me for feeling I am unimportant and that the job You have given me is insignificant. I know I am just like a dust rag, cut to exactly the right size for You to use. I want to be soft to Your voice in my heart. Please spray me with the Holy Spirit, and help me wipe all the surfaces of my life and others' lives clean today. I am praising You, dear Jesus. Amen.

My Cleaning Supplies/Habits Journal

"I promise to work on this project and not take on the organization of any other room until my tools and cleaning supplies are sorted and stored properly."

1. Circle or name three major problems with your cleaning supplies or habits, prioritizing them with numbers.

   - Cleaning tools are not centrally located
   - Supplies are too far from bathroom and kitchen
   - Supplies are mingled with other items (laundry, household tools, etc.)
   - Cleaning products are not safely stored
   - Unused surplus supplies have accumulated
   - No cleaning routine or schedule
   - Limited or no help from family members
   - Other:

   ____

   ____

2. Because I know He cares if my home is clean, my prayer for God's customized solution is the following:

   ____

   ____

   ____

3. The Scripture that has encouraged me to organize these cleaning supplies and habits is the following:

   ____

   ____

4. In order to complete my prioritized tasks, the supplies that I will need or the changes I need to make are the following:

   - Three containers for Trash, Donate, Save
   -
   -
   -

(This is a good time to read and follow "It's Time to Organize That Cleaning Supplies/Closet.")

5. (*To be completed when cleaning supplies are orderly and new cleaning schedule has been practiced for 2 weeks.*)
   I see that God helped me accomplish sorting my supplies, relocating some of them, and trying to form new cleaning routines. Some changes I made are the following (include today's date):

6. My *one year later* journal entry about my cleaning habits and supplies is (include the date):

It's Time to Organize Those Cleaning Supplies/Closet

In this project, the main goal will be the *convenient yet concealed* location of supplies and tools. Later we will evaluate cleaning habits or schedules. Before we can discuss the supplies, we must prepare a proper place to store them.

You have read my mind! Get those three containers: Trash, Donate, Save.

Cleaning Closet

Do you have a *central closet* to contain all or most of your cleaning tools and supplies? If you do, let's start there. If this closet has been used for other purposes, purge and store all non-cleaning items elsewhere. Gather all the common tools you use for cleaning. Now we will sort them by sizes and uses.

Where or how will I store all of my tools in this closet?

Walls

Install wall hangers to hold brooms, dustpans, mops, long-handled tools. These hangers are a minimal expense.

This may be a good place to hang a storage holder for plastic or paper grocery bags and trash bags. Recycle all unnecessary bags. You only need a small supply since you constantly bring home more.

Shelves

This closet should have one or two shelves for storage of small items in bins. Store new light bulbs here in sturdy plastic bins labeled for regular and specialty light bulbs. Using one shallow shelf would allow for the storage of tall handles of brooms, etc. beneath it with easier access.

A bin with a small set of common household tools would be handy here along with a few screws, nails and picture hangers, and a small hammer.

Floor

If floor space allows, store the vacuum in this central location. On the shelf or on hooks, store vacuum bags, vacuum replacement belts, and vacuum tools if yours are not "on board" the vacuum. These small accessories can go on the shelf, in a bin, or be hung on a hook.

If your closet is large and you have other floor cleaning tools, place them here. (Example: carpet shampooer)

If you do not have a central closet, find locations for these objects near the areas to be cleaned:

- Broom and dustpan near kitchen
- Mop near kitchen
- Vacuum and accessories in closet near living room
- Small bins of items can be located under a sink, in a kitchen cabinet or in a "mud room" cabinet.

Cleaning Supplies

Keep all cleaning products in a *convenient yet safe location.*

In general, most of us own too many cleaning products. Gather yours from all over the house and purge those that are not effective.

If possible, keep bathroom cleaning products in or near the bathroom(s). This will save a lot of steps.

If possible, store a tote with weekly cleaning products

for the entire house such as furniture polish, rags, feather dusters, window cleaner, and a toothbrush for cleaning small grooves, etc.

If your central cleaning closet has enough space, store dangerous drain cleaners, and other hazardous products on the highest shelf.

Now, empty those three containers. Old cleaning products placed in the "Trash" need to be evaluated and tightly sealed. If there is *any* question about toxic contents, call a Poison Prevention Hot Line to get instructions. There should be little in your "Donate" container unless you have several duplicated tools or some tools you never use. Sort through your "Save" box, dispersing items throughout the house or possibly the garage.

Cleaning Habits

Let's take a brief moment to discuss your cleaning habits. Do you realize that you are in the position of "homemaker" but that you may not have been trained for this job? Or even with training, you are not really good at it? Now is the time to really evaluate these essentials of cleaning and to do the job with excellence. It will take an evaluation of and commitment to these basics: supplies, schedules, and support.

- *Supplies:* As noted before, you only need a few essential tools and supplies: a good vacuum, a broom, dustpan, a duster, sponges, sink cleaners, an antiseptic compound (even bleach works), a cleaning compound (Examples: Murphy's, Formula 409, Fantastic, etc.), a polish. Less really is better.

A PERSONAL CLEANING HINT

Do you ever consider your dishwasher a cleaning tool? I never did until I discovered that it is great to sanitize sponges and clean stove parts like grates, trays, and pans. I set it to the china cycle and wash all the knick-knacks, vases, or other glass objects that otherwise would require my standing at the sink to rinse the dust off them. This is a great time-saver!

- *Schedule:* If you have a job, you are expected to report to work on specific days in order to accomplish your tasks. Housekeeping/cleaning should be no different. Actually, it is easier if you make a routine "appointment" with yourself to dig in and get the job done. Try a once-a-week schedule of going through the bathrooms, vacuuming, dusting (if needed), mopping the kitchen, cleaning entry floors, and changing the beds. With a family still at home, this may be easier to do if divided into two sessions: beds and bedrooms on one day, the rest of the house on another. Or if you have a home with two or three levels, do the main floor one day, the other two levels on another day. Whatever plan you devise, try your best to *get a flow or routine to cleaning* the house weekly. Clutter will be decreased, the atmosphere will be calmer, and you will begin to sense control over your house instead of it controlling you.

ANOTHER PERSONAL CLEANING HINT

Let's talk about *lists.* I am a great list-maker. I love lists!

But I am painfully aware that not everyone "lives in Judy's world." Perhaps lists will not work for you, but try it anyway. You can use them for a general, weekly list of cleaning jobs. They will *help you stay on task* and give you pleasure when the cleaning is finished. As you get better in accomplishing your cleaning goals, you may add extras that you want to do each week like cleaning your purse or sorting a few photos or sweeping the garage. Start out with the basic necessities to maintain your home, and then branch out only after you see you are able do more.

The other time I make a list is when I do the twice-yearly deep cleaning, in the fall and in the spring. I make this list room-by-room, starting at the top with cobwebs and ceilings, finishing at the bottom baseboards. Specific areas are unique to each room like game closets or coffee table drawers or fireplace hearths. I list these special duties so I do not forget them. As each room is completely cleaned, only then do I move on to the next room. If you want, put this list into the computer or a notebook so you do not have to rethink it each season.

- *Support:* Enlist your "troops" to help in this schedule. First find a day or evening that works for most of the family. If necessary, assign specific jobs (age appropriate) to your children. Even small children can take a rag and wipe dust from their bed frame and surrounding tables as they put away toys. Older children can help in the bathrooms (check chemical safety) and family areas. My husband is the best vacuum pusher in the world! If it were not for him, my carpet would be continuously scattered with debris. Ask your spouse what job he thinks he could do to help you. When working together, it is surprising how little time it actually takes to clean a house. Put on a little good music, and set a timer. Even jobs you hate doing don't really take that long. Done regularly, the cleaning goes faster and makes the house easier to maintain.

Give Credit to the Lord

Now that you have moved all cleaning tools and products to *convenient, concealed, and safe* locations and evaluated your cleaning habits, take time to thank the Lord for giving you a plan to do this.

Dear Lord, thank You for giving me special guidance in the storage of my cleaning tools and products. I thank You that because of this organization, I will be able to keep my home cleaner and safer, not wasting as much time doing it. Thank You for showing me how to clean on a regular basis and not let this task overwhelm me. Please help me to use this clean home for Your honor. I pray these things in the name of Jesus. Amen

Now go back a few pages and complete *My Cleaning Supplies/Habits Journal.*

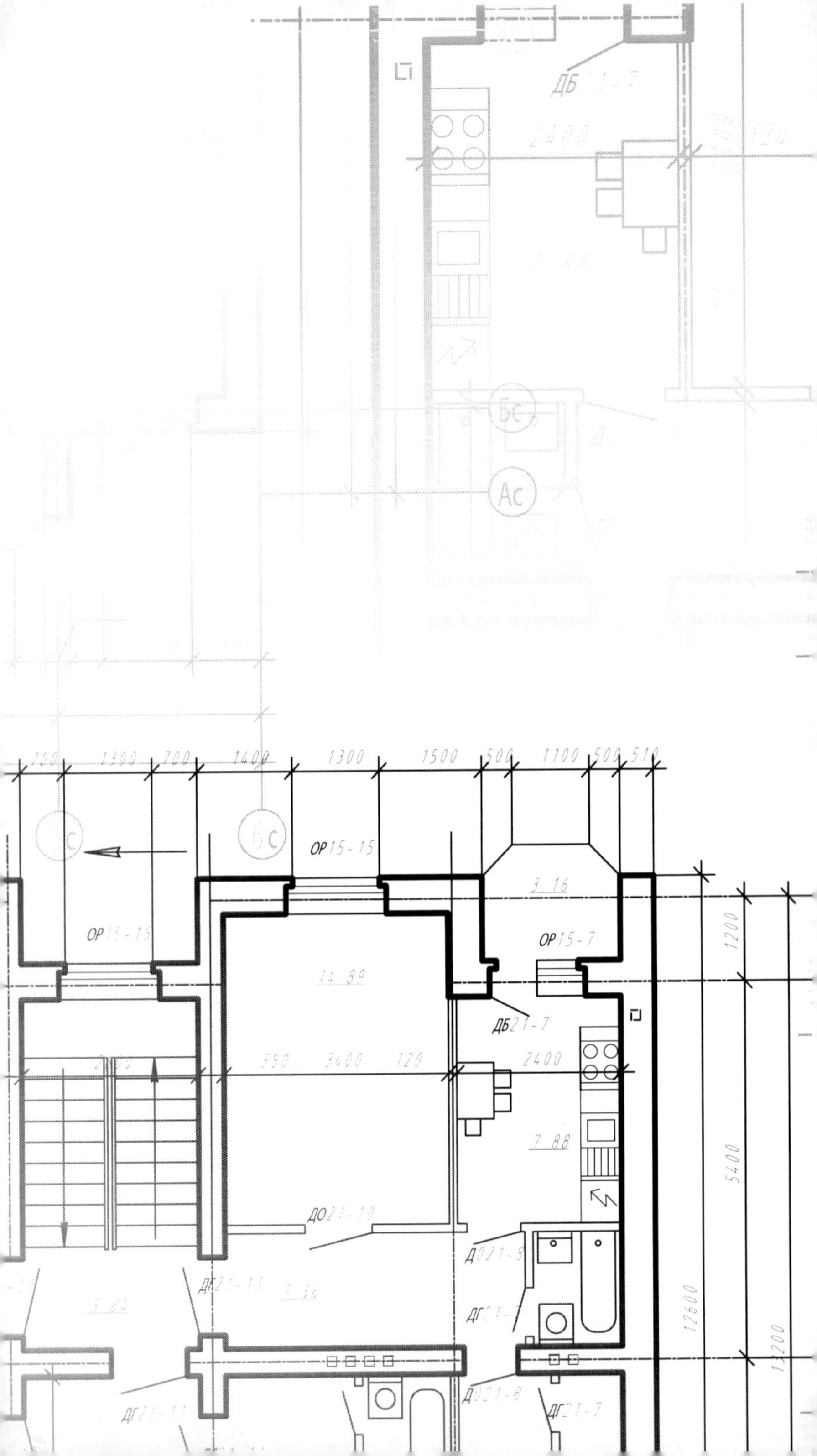

700
1300
700
1400
1300
1500
500
1100
500
510
ОР15-15
ОР15-15
3.16
ОР15-7
1200
14.89
ДБ21-7
330
3400
120
2400
7.88
5400
ДО21-10
ДО21-8
ДГ21-11
7.36
3.64
ДГ21-
12600
13200
ДГ21-11
ДО21-8
ДГ21-7

Shoeboxes and Other Low Cost Filing Systems

The Office/Study/Photos

So, why do you think that you cannot file your papers or keep your photos in order? For most people, they lack a *system to use on a consistent basis.* It needs to be ongoing, long-term, and able to be changed or refined to meet changing needs. That is also part of the problem—our needs are always changing. One thing that should be a constant is that we have a file into which we put our papers. It does not need to be fancy or intricate, just plain and easy. You can alphabetize or categorize, but decide on a system, and then start using it. You will be amazed at how little time it actually takes to sort those papers and file them once you get started.

So, why would God care how we take care of our papers? He has given us all that we have, and He has also given us all the money to buy all that we have. Don't you think that He cares that we keep the guarantees and receipts in order? Did He provide you with a home or an apartment? Then, He cares that you keep the mortgage agreement and payment files up to date. Did He give you a car? Then He cares if the tire guarantee is still good when one tire is defective. Did He give you a good camera? Then He cares if all the memories captured on that camera are kept for your enjoyment and for your ancestors. He cares because *He intends to guard* all that He has already given you.

By studying His Word and asking for His help in creating a good filing system, you will be able to meet the challenge of putting all of those papers and photos in order. Take the challenge. Begin by studying God's Word and praying over those files and photos.

O dear Lord, You know that all the paperwork in this home really makes me feel overwhelmed. Please help me find a way to put filing, photos, and correspondence in order so that we may actually use all of it. You know my frustrations in the past with not being able to find important documents when I need them. You also know that the most important worldly possessions I have are my photos. Please bring less stress to this home because of Your help with this organizing project. Thank You for Your direction. Amen.

"God loves us not because of who we are
but because of who God is."[6]

Philip Yancey

Job Security for a Shredder

Junk Mail

But Moses said to God, "Who am I, that I should go to Pharaoh, and that I should bring the sons of Israel out of Egypt?" And He said, "Certainly I will be with you, and this shall be the sign to you that it is I who have sent you: when you have brought the people out of Egypt you shall worship God at this mountain."

—Exodus 3:11–12

Junk mail has become much more sophisticated in the past few years due to computers. Instead of "occupant," the letters now bear your name, often in bold, black print. The most thrilling junk mail is the annual barrage of sweepstakes entries.

Almost daily a new sweepstakes letter arrives, announcing "You Are a Guaranteed Winner" followed by the small print stating "if your name is drawn." My guaranteed winnings now stand roughly at $3,640,225.00 . . . if my name is ever drawn! But then there are the difficult decisions like whether to take the cash or the dream house or the luxury car/world tour combination. My chances of winning are one in thirteen million so I told the mailman to be sure to sound his horn when he delivers my "You Are a Grand Prize Winner" letter. At the price of postage, I figure within a few years I will have spent enough to buy *him* the luxury car and could have taken the world tour first class myself!

Out of all the millions of responses, who am I to ever be chosen a "winner"? How similarly outnumbered Moses felt when God chose him to be the leader of the children of Israel. Out of all the Jews, why would God choose him? He looked within himself, looked at his shortcomings, felt inadequate, and asked, "Who am I . . . ?"

Do you ever feel that way when you know God is calling you to do a certain job? Why me? From all these Christians in this church or in this world, why me? What do I have that would be as good as or better than someone else? So quickly we forget God's promise to be with us in whatever we do for Him.

The life of the Christian is the biggest sweepstakes anyone can ever enter. There are limitless chances, "bonuses," and guaranteed "prizes." Is God calling you to a certain job right now? Is He tugging at your heart to serve Him? Instead of offering excuses as Moses did, send God your "yes" answers. Consider how He has prepared you for the job He is calling you to do and determine to be a "winner."

O God, my heavenly Father, I feel like Moses and ask you, "Who am I" that You are leading me, calling me to do a job for which I feel too small? Looking at my past, I know You have been preparing me for this service, and I claim Your promise to guide and strengthen me to do it. I will do it by Your help and grace. I know that doing this will cause me to grow and will increase my faith and dependence on You. Thank You for trusting me to choose to be Your servant. In the name of Jesus, I pray. Amen.

The Presence of the Past

The Photo Album

I will rejoice greatly in the Lord, my soul will exult in my God; for He has clothed me with garments of salvation, He has wrapped me with a robe of righteousness, as a bridegroom adorns himself with a garland, and as a bride adorns herself with her jewels. For as the earth brings forth its sprouts, and as the garden causes the things sown in it to spring up, so the Lord God will cause righteousness and praise to spring up before all the nations.

—Isaiah 61:10–11

And the Spirit and the bride say, "Come." And let the one who hears say, "Come." And let the one who is thirsty come; let the one who wishes take the water of life without cost.

—Revelation 22:17

It's a simple tradition that we have, but so meaningful. Each year, during the week of our anniversary, we find the "Wedding Album" and look at all the memories captured there. We recite the events to our children and tell them about those first years before they were in our life. It was a simple engagement and wedding. College costs were our main concern, not extra money for us.

That first apartment near campus had a shared bathroom. That's right. We shared it with the tenant in the next apartment. We decided after just a few months that we could share a *lot* of things, but *not* our bathroom anymore. The next two apartments were rented from a man who looked just like the bald, muscular man on the Mr. Clean bottle. And keep those apartments clean he did!

There were a few more years of renting, but things gradually improved. First, we got an apartment with our own bathroom! Then, we later rented a duplex and finally a whole house. College was finally finished. Shortly after the birth of our children, we purchased a home, a better car, and took a few vacations. Time seems to bring an enrichment of family, possessions, and careers. We thank the Lord for this progression each time we review the past.

What a contrast this is to our standing in Christ. We do not have to work for Him all of our lives to earn a home with Him. The moment we say, "I do" to Christ, we are immediately given all that He has. We have a home with Him, riches immeasurable, blessings unspeakable, peace unending, and love unwavering. He gives to us His whole being and all that is His from that first moment—no increase or decrease ever.

Oh, that we could reminisce often about our "marriage" to Him and appreciate all that He gives to us from that instant through eternity. Open God's "photo album," the Bible, God's love letter to us. Review verses that remind you of what He has done. He has given us Himself.

Dear Lord Jesus, I remember right now that moment that I said, "I do," "yes," to Your gift of forgiveness and accepted You as my personal Savior. How this thrills my heart to remember that moment, that day. Renew my zeal for You, dear Jesus. I still love You, and I love You even more than on that day because I now appreciate Your gift to me. Keep this memory sharp in my mind. Amen.

"As long as you can sweeten another's pain, life is not in vain."[7]

Helen Keller

SWAK
Stationery

You are our letter, written in our hearts, known and read by all men; being manifested that you are a letter of Christ, cared for by us, written not with ink, but with the Spirit of the living God, not on tablets of stone, but on tablets of human hearts.

—II Corinthians 3:2–3

I opened it excitedly, like everyone else opens Christmas presents. Oh, a new box of pink stationery with tiny bouquets of pink roses tied with a wisp of blue ribbon. Each stack of note cards and envelopes was bound with thin, pink sashes. What a perfect gift! My sister-in-law certainly knew I could use and would appreciate this gift that would help me in my weekly efforts to span the gulf of distance between our families. I would probably remember her with each sheet I used. Yet I cannot pick up my pen to write a letter without remembering the verses above.

Every day, we are writing a letter with our life. Its pages are open for all around us to read. We may not like to write letters, but this one we write without even being conscious of it. Our words, deeds, and actions are being inscribed on the "paper" which is our life. Our attitudes, priorities, love, hate, etc. leave a lasting picture or legacy. Some write beautiful words on ugly, torn paper or on a shattered life. Some write wicked words on beautiful paper or on a life blessed with a beautiful body, yet darkness is under that surface. Some write boring words on manila paper and seal it in a manila envelope, the picture of a life lived in laziness and apathy. All write with ink, no erasures possible. Yet all may use the blotter, our Savior's precious blood, to remove the mess and guilt our smudged ink has made. The Savior sees only a blank where that deed was. But still, our words and deeds will remain behind us for all others to see, our legacy.

Are you interested in only leaving a short e-mail message to all who know you, or are you interested in leaving a detailed, personally handwritten letter with your life? How is your "letter" coming?

My dear Father, I realize my life is open and being "read" by everyone around me. I am not sure that I am proud of it or that I am writing Your wonderful love letters in my words and actions. Will You help me see myself today as a letter being written by You to others? Please help me write Your beautiful love into my "letter," my legacy. I thank You in Jesus' name for this picture. Amen.

"Consider the postage stamp; its usefulness consists in the ability to stick to one thing till it gets there."

Josh Billings

My Office/Study/Photo Journal

"I promise to work on this room and not take on the organization of any other room until my files, office, and photos are in proper order."

It would be difficult for the most organized person to tackle organizing their office and files as well as their photos at the same time. So let's treat these as separate organizing tasks. For that reason, the office/study/photo areas will be easier to journal if you make separate lists for your problems and your progress.

Office/Study Journal

1. Circle or name three major problem areas in the management of your filing (bills and receipts)/office/study area, prioritizing them with numbers:

    - Lack of proper equipment (file unit with drawers, desk, shredder, folders, etc.)
    - No filing system or habits
    - Files are in disarray
    - Overwhelmed by junk mail
    - No central bill/mailing center
    - No area to store correspondence or greeting cards
    - Receipts and documents are not filed; hard to retrieve
    - Bills are hard to find and often paid late
    - Other:

____

____

2. Because I know He intends to help me care for all He has given to me, my prayer for His customized solution is the following:

____

____

____

3. The Scripture that has encouraged me to organize my files and office is the following:

____

____

____

4. In order to complete my prioritized tasks, the supplies I will need are the following:

   - Three containers for Trash, Donate, Save
   -
   -
   -

(This is a good time to read and follow "It's Time to Organize That Office/Study Area.")

5. *(To be completed after your files/office/study organizing job is finished.)*
   I see that God helped me accomplish organizing this important area of my life. My feelings about my office now are (include today's date)

____

____

6. My *one year later* journal about the files and our office area is (include the date):

Photo Storage Journal

1. Circle or name three major problems with your photo storage, prioritizing them with numbers.

    - Photos are in envelopes or boxes, unsorted
    - Photos are in albums, but poorly arranged or unlabeled
    - Some photos are on CDs but there's no uniform storage or cataloging of them
    - There is no plan for future photos
    - The cost of electronic transfer of photos has delayed my organization
    - Other:

2. Because I know God wants me to preserve these most precious memories in the best way possible, my prayer for His customized solution is the following:

3. The Scripture that has encouraged me to organize my photos is the following:

4. In order to complete my prioritized tasks, the supplies that I will need to store my photos are the following:

(This would be a good time to read and follow along with the suggested organization of photos in the "It's Time to Organize That Office/Study" chapter of this book.)

5. (To be completed after your photos are sorted and organized.)
   I see that God helped me sort and organize my photos. My feelings and plans for these and future photos are as follows (include today's date):

6. My *one year later* journal entry about my photos is (include the date):

It's Time to Organize That

Office/Study/Photo Area

In general, paper clutter is the most frustrating part of trying to maintain an organized, tidy house. It is a *daily, multi-family member* problem. Listed below will be the areas paper clutter comes into the home and some of the *best* ways to contain it. You may not need an entire study or den to handle it, but you will need a designated area to sort and file papers and photos in order to find them in the future. Brush up on your alphabetizing skills, and let's get shredding!

Wait! Don't forget those three containers for "Save," "Donate," and "Trash." Also get a paper shredder ready for papers that have account numbers, old bank records, or social security numbers. Let's go.

Mail

If you don't do it already, open all mail over the trash can (or over a paper shredder).

- *Be ruthless.* Decide as it is opened if you really want to entertain any new credit card offers, store offers, flyers, or catalogs.
- *You must know your budget.* If it is when you feel you are able to spend or need to improve some percentage interest rates, save some offers. If it is a time to be frugal with your income, throw it all out and don't tempt yourself.
- *Catalogs.* Here is where the quantity of junk mail begins to pile up. *Make a decision to throw away catalogs* and do the looking on the internet. At the most, I tear out a page from a

catalog and then research the item online. Most often, I find I really don't need it and can buy something as good or better at a lower price locally. *If* you do keep some catalogs, keep only the ones you regularly order from and keep only the current issue, tossing the older ones.

- *This is the general rule for junk mail:* each offer and catalog will be duplicated in a short time *so trash it.*

Bills

This is a good time to discuss a *bill paying/mail center.* Please do not use one of the wall mounted racks to hold bills. The whole wall looks cluttered. You want a new *center,* not a rack.

Find a desk with a drawer, or a small rack to contain bills, or a bin will work. In this desk area/center you will want to have the following:

- Calculator
- Postage stamps
- Return address labels or stamp
- Pens, pencils
- Envelopes
- Paper clips
- Stapler

As the bills arrive, place them immediately in the *back* of the bills to pay. The reason for this is that the *oldest due dates will stay to the front of the pile.*

A PERSONAL ORGANIZING EXAMPLE:

One of my dearest clients was having a problem getting her bills paid on time and thus incurring several late fees per month, not to mention a worsening credit rating. I asked her to show me her method of paying bills and her area to work on bills. She retrieved a shoebox and said she just worked at the kitchen table, storing all the necessary stamps, etc. in kitchen drawers. I asked her what she did when a bill comes in the mail. Her reply: "I throw it in the top of the shoebox." It was evident that her system, as simple as a shoebox sounds, was workable. I just needed an equally simple solution. Wow! I had just come from work where we had rows and rows of filing cabinets and computers to write our checks and keep our schedules accurate. How could I work with a shoebox? I gave a quick prayer to the Lord to bless my mind with simplicity yet accuracy. Immediately, the word "top" came to mind and we reviewed her procedure to store incoming mail. Yes, she just needed to place each new bill in the *bottom* of the box keeping the oldest on the top. Then, when she went to pay them, she would be paying the oldest first, thus avoiding late fees and poor credit. Isn't God able to care for our bills from the top to the bottom? Doesn't He love to simplify our lives right down to a shoebox? God loves the simple!

Filing

All right, you can now get the bills paid on time. What happens next? Where do you store the "stubs," receipts, and records that you need to save? My attitude is that files have to be workable, not hard work. Let's make that happen!

For home filing, simply get a *small,* alphabetical, accordion file to put records into on the day of bill paying. It is understandable that you cannot work in your large, permanent record files each week or two; however, you can easily move payment records every couple of months from this *small folder* to your regular system.

A Temporary Filing System

After the bills are paid, I suggest using the small, alphabetical, accordion file for *temporary* use. The temporary file will *match your permanent records,* but is portable and smaller:

A=Automobile. Keep records of your auto care or purchases here: brake job, tire guarantees, oil changes, etc.

B=Banking receipts. Place your checking account reconciliation statements, deposit slips, bank/mortgage records, etc.

C=Credit Card statements and agreements *or* Certificates (birth, auto, etc.)

D=Debit receipts (can throw out after bank reconciliation) or Dog/vet bills

E=Energy bill receipts (these are not really necessary to keep unless you are tracking your energy use long-term or dispute readings)

F="Family" records or use something that helps your filing

G=Guarantees. This would incorporate *sales receipts* since they are our guarantee to return merchandise. Also, you will need to keep guarantees of all sorts with the *sales receipt for that item stapled to it.* Miscellaneous sales receipts could be purged every two to three months.

H=Health records for the family

I=Insurance. The actual policies will not fit into this small folder; however, you can keep current premium renewals here. This is best used for all insurances *except* medical insurance papers. (It could also be used for Investments.)

M=Medical related (doctor receipts, prescription, premiums, etc.)

R=Retirement.

T=Tax related (forms, receipts, church statements, deduction receipts, etc.)

V=Vacation plans or vacation reservations

You certainly will have things that fit under some of these headings and others that will remain empty.

Just remember to move the records from this small folder into your permanent files in approximately two month intervals so it does not get overwhelming. The idea of it is that your receipts are not just stacked haphazardly, but you will be able to find it as needed even for the short-term.

Permanent/Long-Standing Files

A good home filing system need *not* be complicated. Keep it simple.

A two-drawer file will be sufficient for most households. The categories can be the *same as in your temporary files* with a few subheadings or file folders arranged alphabetically within the categories. This would be a good example: *Insurance* category with file folders titled and in alphabetical order such as: *A*uto, *H*ouse, *Life,* and

Medical. These folders would contain the large policies and current premium payment records.

A PERSONAL ORGANIZING SUGGESTION VITAL TO YOUR FILES

Below are two all-important files that I want you to put at the front of the top filing drawer:

First, *get a red folder.* This will be your emergency, all-the-information-in-a-nutshell folder that will be at the *front of your top file* drawer. *It will contain the most vital of all information in your household* and will be ready to be accessed at a moment's notice. Here is what you put in it:

Empty your wallet and your spouse's wallet. *Photocopy* all credit cards, Social Security cards, medical cards, and any other photo identification. Now turn each over and photocopy the back sides. The back side contains the phone numbers of credit card companies to report theft. These copies are vital to your identity. Now remove the Social Security card placing it in a safe or safe deposit box at the bank. *Do not carry your Social Security card with you at any time.*

Add to this red folder a paper with the names and phone numbers of family members to be notified if there is an emergency. This paper could be valuable to friends or sitters in the event of an accident. Add one more paper to this file, one that lists the location of important documents such as life insurance policy, living trust papers, the names of your doctors, bank names, and location of titles to vehicles, etc. This folder should contain about three major informational papers.

Second, *get a green folder.* This will represent money. Use this for an ongoing receipt folder for *income tax.* Routinely drop in church receipts, tax receipts, some medical receipts, anything related to your income tax for the current year. Many organizers will tell you to sort these weekly or monthly, but we all know that will not happen. But you can separate these receipts (using your small accordion file) as they are received and have the proper records ready on January 1st each year. All that will be left to do at that point would be to categorize them and deliver them to the tax preparer. Remember what I said: *Files have to be workable, not hard work.*

Banking Information

Divide into banks if you use more than one. Keep each bank's records in a separate file folder.

Divide banking records into categories such as deposit slips, statements, and mortgage records.

Credit Card Records

Keep not only the statements, but the *original agreements* that state interest rates, billing rules, late payment fees, etc. You may need these if you ever dispute charges.

Employment Records

Keep contracts, pension plans, company information, related study certificates.

Guarantees

Divide guarantees into categories: Electronic (cameras, computers, etc.), Garage or Workshop (large power tools like saws, drills, small tools, anything used in these areas), Household (appliances, fixtures, vacuums, building materials such as a guarantee for an exterior door, etc.), Landscaping/Garden (mowers, yard tools, etc.). Keep your categories in alphabetical order.

Health

Make a firm decision whether to file personal medical records, health insurance, and medical resource files here or under a category titled "medical." It will be confusing to have two categories. Whether you do it here or in "medical," create a folder for each family member to retain shot records, lab results, etc. Also create a resource file for articles of information on diseases that relate to your family. If desired, medical insurance papers can be kept here, but I do not recommend it.

Insurances

Divide into *auto* insurance policies, *house* insurance policies, *life* insurance policies, and any other that you may have. If desired, medical insurance can be in this file; however, I prefer a separate file for this category.

Medical

This file should be kept for the *coverage and cost records* of medical care. Keep your insurance carrier's booklet(s) or policy copies here. It is also a good place to reference on-going claims. There are usually several papers issued on claims that must be retained and cross-referenced when there are denials and payments. There are usually pharmacy receipts or prescription details as well as other related cost papers that must be retained that may or may not be retained for tax purposes.

Pending File

This would be a file of issues awaiting other paperwork, but not urgent. Medical or insurance claims or *comparison offers* for future consideration for cell phones, cable channels, or satellite television would be good examples of "pending" issues.

Tax Related

(Do this if you decide *not* to use the green folder in front of file drawer)

This can be an ongoing file of receipts for items that you know are tax deductions: property tax receipts, medical insurance/health care receipts, pay stubs, etc. This is the place to keep the name of your accountant or tax preparer as well as any instructions or information they give you.

A COLORFUL, PERSONAL NOTE

I recently color-coded my files at a minimal cost. Already categorized and then alphabetized, I revamped the categories with colored hanging files and matching colored folders. The results are that at a glance, I can recognize my banking, investment, and income section (green/money), medical section (red/important), travel membership section (blue/restful), home services such as cable, phone (yellow/happy). Do you see the relationship to the colors? Try it! It works!

If you are not able to purchase new, colored folders and hanging files, try colored labeling tapes to use in your label-maker or use colored ink in your computer generated labels. You will see your categories just "pop."

Correspondence Area

The best arrangement would be keeping this area near your mailing/bill paying center. If that's not possible, find a desk or large drawer to hold your correspondence materials.

Keep one section for greeting cards, one for note cards, one for envelopes, and one for stationery. If possible, keep stamps and return address labels here also.

Computer Desk

There are so many small items that support your computer, you will need to think about a nearby, neat area to hold these items. If you do not have a cupboard or a large computer desk, a plastic, rolling drawer unit may hold all you need. It will hold:

- Ink cartridges
- Large paper supplies
- Labels
- Manuals
- New CDs
- Miscellaneous

There are now so many good storage items for computer-related use that you can consider these. If it is possible to keep it at *eye level and above,* that would eliminate desk-level clutter.

Now take time to go back a few pages and complete the Office/Study Journal section of the *Office/Study/Photo Journal.*

Photos

Here are two facts about photos:

1. They are without a doubt the *most precious, valuable* items we own.
2. We have too many of them.

Without exception, if our home was on fire the only thing we should run to save other than our family would be our photos. They cannot be replaced. But they are never protected nor are they easily "grabbed" when the house is on fire. How can we bring this overwhelming collection of the most precious memories we have under control? Perhaps my own experience will help you see that it can be done.

A PERSONAL ORGANIZING STORY

Answering questions after speaking to a local group of ladies, one woman posed her problem of unsorted, unlabeled, volumes of photos. I glibly replied, "I must admit, I have the same problem, but I've decided I'll organize them when I am only able to stay home all the time and not do things like this!" Afterward, I felt like a colossal failure. Not only had I left her with no way to find a remedy, I was admitting to being a hypocrite. If anyone had seen my boxes and books of unlabeled, unsorted photos, they would certainly have questioned my "professional" organizing credentials.

The Lord really convicted me of my need to use my skills and stop just giving lip-service to my organizing clients and guests. But how would I organize years of these photos? Many were poorly arranged in old albums that had yellowing plastic pages. Most were not labeled or dated. Only a big God could direct the clearing of this big mess! After pulling out each album, folder, box and bag of photos, I was humbled by the value of this collection. I gave the Lord thanks for the cameras, thanks for my photographer-husband, thanks for my parents, thanks for my children and friends and vacations and beautiful sunsets. I asked for a new, easy method to put it all in order. My mind was repeatedly directed to the sorting of a cluttered room: put like objects together.

After writing each person's name on a sheet of copy paper, I followed with others labeled "friends," "extended family," "vacations," etc. Then I began my system of dealing photos as if I was employed in a casino. There was no reason to shuffle my "decks of photos." They were already in disarray.

Once the photos were in personal stacks, I was challenged to identify the dates. As I arranged them in chronological order, it became easy to identify events and therefore, put a year-date or sometimes even a month-and-year-date on each photo. Each chronological stack was put into a photo box and the rest has been easy. Many have made it to albums and are already passed on to my children to enjoy.

What pleasure we have found as a family by preserving and sharing these precious memories of toothless grins, Christmas gatherings, graduations, trained chicken pets, first bike rides and loving grandparents. What pleasure God must derive when He gives us a specific answer to a specific problem and we benefit from listening and acting on that answer. By resolving my photo problem, God showed me another "picture" of Himself.

You are not the only person who doesn't have beautiful photo albums to display or all your photos stored on CDs in your computer. It can be done! You really can conquer the mess. Start with a prayer for a clear vision to solve this problem and then follow these *starter tips.* The *completion of albums or organized electronic storage will be your long-term goal.*

Gather

Gather all photos from every corner of the house. If you know your old albums have the type of plastic film that will deteriorate your photos, empty all of these albums. Use a large table to hold all that you have gathered. This will make an excellent sorting area.

Sort

There will be a *general sorting* and then an *individual sorting*

Once all photos are gathered, it is time to sort. I prefer sorting by *person* and then by event or essentially, *chronological order.*

General Sorting of Photos

Start sorting with these headings:

- Each immediate family member
- Group family photos
- Extended family photos
- Dear friends
- Vacations or travels

If you are unable to continue and need to store these photos until your next sorting session, I suggest using large, manila envelopes labeled with the person's name, or "Dear Friends," etc. *Stand* these envelopes in a large plastic tub or a solid box so "labels" are easily seen. This will make it easier for you to just sit down and pick it back up where you stopped.

Individual Sorting of Photos

- Take just one individual's photos and begin to *sort chronologically:* birth, toddler, preschool, first school days, preteens, high school, graduation, college, graduation, engagement/fiancé, marriage, birth of children.
- The chronological order will begin to bring *events* into groupings.
- If you are not ready to put these into a new album, purchase a photo box for each family member's photos and make dividers indicating chronological order as listed above.
- This sorting will enable you to readily find the photo you are looking for later and will help you place them in albums.
- For extended family photos and dear friends, just sort by person and/or couple, and then sort chronologically, just as you did for individual photos. You will see them over a time period this way.
- For vacations or travels, just sort by place or trip. Note the year you traveled or took the vacation, and put any details on the back of the photos.

Storage

If they never make it to an album, they are in order by person, event, dates, and relationships. Pretty, labeled, matching photo boxes with dividers will do until you can put these into albums. The box dividers can also serve to identify timelines, ages, and events relating to your photos. You will be able to locate any photo in a moment by having gathered and sorted all of your photos.

If you are a computer-friendly person and not desiring to ever have your photos in albums, check with your local stores for ideas on how to store your photos on a CD or DVD. There are stores that provide this service, and once your photos are in order, it would be easy to turn them over to this service to be processed into this space-saving storage.

Future Photos

Now that you have the entire photo history of your family, friends, and travels in order, it will just be a matter of adding to this history by placing recent photos in the proper boxes. If you have been able to place this history in albums, new albums can be continued or added to the old ones. For those who choose the electronic storage of photos, adding new photos by your computer will be easy since they are already in chronological order.

If done on a continuing basis, the maintenance of your family photo history will not be overwhelming.

Give Credit to the Lord

Do you realize the size of the project that you have just completed? Give great thanks for the Lord's help!

Dear Lord, I am just so thankful You have given me the energy and ability to organize my files, my photos and my office areas. You know how much stress this has caused every time I could not find necessary papers. Thank You, Lord, and I pray that You will give me the ability to keep my papers filed and my photos in order. You know that those photos hold the memories of my family and a history of what You have blessed us with... each other. You have been my strength through this whole task. Amen.

Now take time to go back a few pages and complete the Photo Journal section of the *Office/Study Area/Photo Journal.*

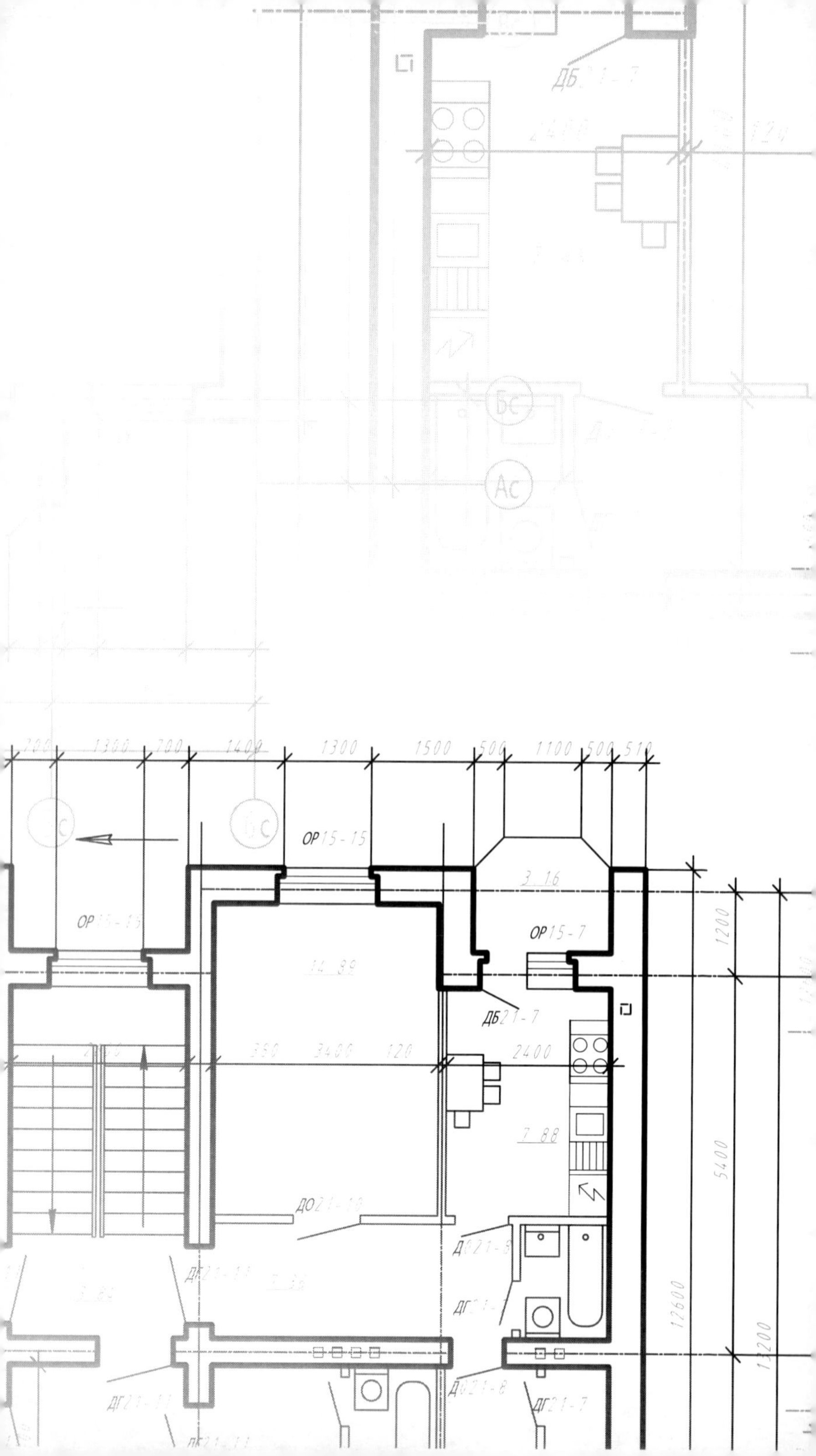

1300
1500
1100
OP15-15
3.16
OP15-7
14.89
ДБ21-7
3400
120
2400
7.88
1200
5400
12600
13200
ДО21-8
ДГ21-7

Overdue, Past Due, and Can't Do!

Finances

"Watch your pennies, and your dollars will take care of themselves," is closer to the truth than any of us care to admit. Plus, it takes discipline to watch how we spend our pennies. That means sticking to a budget, tithing, investing for our future, and not wasting money on impulse purchases and all those other "accounting things" that really don't appeal to us. Well, if possessions and money were not important to God, He would not have talked about them in 2,350 verses in the Bible.[8] Our money *is* important to Him. But along with the blessing of an income, He expects us to use our gift of money wisely. Just as we cannot jump on the sofa He has given us, we cannot waste money or mishandle it and expect this blessing to continue to be of use.

So, how do we organize our finances? How do we get bills paid on time? You are probably not an accountant and for that matter, may not even like to do math. Is it *really* that hard? Trust me, you can do it! If we first discuss this with the Lord, seek a good plan, and lay our bills out in an organized fashion, God will disclose an answer to us. We need prayer and commitment over this task. Let's get started.

Dear Jesus, so many times in the New Testament You talk about our money. I know I can improve a lot in handling it, and I know that You have expectations of me in the use of it. I know that every dollar I have comes from You. Help me through these meditations and helpful hints to organize my budget and pay my bills on time. Teach me how to save money yet be generous and have a good reputation with others by being honest and upright with the money with which You have blessed me. I thank You for the wisdom and knowledge You are going to give me concerning my finances. Amen.

Cartwheels of Inflation

Grocery Shopping

Or do you not know that your body is a temple of the Holy Spirit who is in you, whom you have from God, and that you are not your own? For you have been bought with a price: therefore glorify God in your body.

—I Corinthians 6:19–20

Years ago when my children were small, grocery shopping was the highlight of my week. It was a good excuse to get out of the house for a while and spend money without too many guilty feelings. With my daughter sitting in the large grocery cart, the baby in the cart seat, and my oldest son hanging onto my jeans, we traveled every aisle. I would spend a whole twenty dollars for the week's supply of groceries and come home in a car bulging with bags of food and happy children clutching animal crackers.

But as you know, inflation has changed this whole scene. Now, for twenty dollars I get four rolls of toilet paper, a can of coffee, six cans of tomato soup, and a bottle of shampoo. Hardly even one bag of groceries. Of course, those little bodies and appetites have inflated right along with the prices.

Graciously, the government has kept us informed of the rate of inflation. Are they trying to depress the entire population of the United States? But good news came last month when they announced that food prices are dropping. I have called and written to every senator and legislator to get the name of the grocery store where they are doing their research. However, this information seems to be more classified than FBI files!

How reassuring to know that "inflation" can never

affect our salvation. Christ paid the price by laying down His holy life in exchange for the punishment that we deserve for our sins. God will never increase or inflate His demand for a holy sacrifice for our sins. The price Christ paid was fixed, final, and in full.

As you shop this week, remember to be thankful for Christ buying you and paying the price for your salvation.

Thank You, our Heavenly Father, for buying eternity for me. What a price You paid in giving Jesus as the sacrifice for my sin. Thank You that You will never demand more than what He has paid for me. My account is settled with You, and I have Your peace. I pray this in the name of my Savior, Jesus Christ. Amen.

Tilt-a-Whirl

The Electric Meter

You shall therefore impress these words of mine on your heart and on your soul; and you shall bind them as a sign on your hand, and they shall be as frontals on your forehead. And you shall teach them to your sons, talking of them when you sit in your house and when you walk along the road and when you lie down and when you rise up. And you shall write them on the door posts of your house and on your gates.

—Deuteronomy 11:18–20

I have to admit I have one real enemy in this world: my electric meter. No matter what I do or don't do, it keeps turning around, adding up more kilowatt hours.

When my family was younger, they gave little cooperation to my "Stop the Meter" campaign. Instead of turning bedroom lights off when leaving for school, they were left burning so the kids could find their rooms at bedtime that night. Hair was never left to dry by itself. Plug in the blow dryer and the curling iron. Cut down on showers? How could three teenagers use less than forty gallons of hot water apiece each morning? When everyone left the room and the television was running, they said they leave it on "just for some noise in the house." When getting potatoes from the basement, the switch was left on because their hands were full. That switch turned on five 100-watt light bulbs.

Asking my husband to turn off some switches at the barn was just too much! If the electric fencer is off, the cattle would get out. If the mercury light was off, he was sure someone would steal from the barn. Was there a big market for "hot hay"?

I offered to do my share, but the family flatly refused

to allow me to sacrifice. I offered to stop washing, stop vacuuming, stop ironing, and stop cooking. So the meter kept running in circles, day after day. I was positive even if I had thrown the main switch off at the breaker box, that meter would have gone right on turning!

As parents, we should be electric meters in our homes. We should be counting, recounting, and telling Christ's great love and promises twenty-four hours a day. By letting God's Word, the current, run through us, we are all charged up to tell everyone we meet of Christ. Even when it seems we are not "plugged in" to our children, we need to keep telling and repeating God's principles and promises.

Inside and outside our homes, in the morning, during work, and at bedtime, they need to know of our love for Christ. Is your meter running? Are you hooked up to the "main power"? Christ has already paid the bill, so use freely!

O dear Father, I need Your power to run through me to my children and everyone who enters this home today. I ask You to impress these words on my heart and soul, keep them on my mind all day. Help me to see every opportunity You put before me to share You, Your truths, Your love. Thank You for paying the price for me with Jesus' blood. Amen.

S-A-L-E, another Four-Letter Word!

Bargain Shopping

The law of the Lord is perfect, restoring the soul; the testimony of the Lord is sure, making wise the simple. The precepts of the Lord are right, rejoicing the heart; the commandment of the Lord is pure, enlightening the eyes. The fear of the Lord is clean, enduring forever; the judgments of the Lord are true and righteous altogether. They are more desirable than gold, yes, than much fine gold; sweeter also than honey and the drippings of the honeycomb.

—Psalm 19:7–10

Not forsaking our own assembling together, as is the habit of some, but encouraging one another, and all the more, as you see the day drawing near.

—Hebrews 10:25

If the U. S. Army could train our men to be as aggressive in war as women are during dollar day sales, every nation in the world would beg us for friendship and mercy! All that pushing, snatching, and shoving is just savage. Worse than the stampede down the aisles is the anticipation a woman goes through before the big sale.

First, check the ads. My husband and I glare at each other through the chopped newspaper. My reply is, "You'll thank me later!" Next, write a careful list with every store, every item, and every price. Those ads are studied so much the print fades.

Now, up early the morning of the sale. What, no time to fix breakfast for the family? They'll survive. I must be on time, even early. I've waited for weeks for this sale, and I'm not going to miss my chance to save a lot of money by spending as much as I can possibly spare . . . and maybe even more!

How different our attitudes can be on some Sunday mornings. It is so easy to give in to feeling so tired or so rushed that we think we should just stay home. We anticipate hearing exactly what we heard last week, see only the same faces, and sing the same old songs. Unlike our shopping sprees, we don't anticipate "purchasing" one new thing. How can we lose our zeal for that which is so vital to our Christian life, yet keep it for things that do nothing to profit us spiritually?

Do our priorities and attitudes need readjusting at times? I think so. Mine do. How is your attitude these days? Are you anticipating bringing home some great "purchase" from your Sunday morning jaunt to church? Let's keep our expectations, excitement, and "purchasing power" high, where it should be.

O dear God, You see my attitudes. Please forgive my wrong attitudes. Help me to be reminded that You are the Great Purchaser. You purchased eternal life for me. O God, help me to be focused on that fact and keep my enthusiasm for You visible to everyone around me. I want to be shopping for sinners today, Lord. Amen.

My Financial Journal

"I promise to work on our financial records, budget, and payments and not take on the organization of any other room until this crucial area of my life is in order."

1. Circle or name three major problem areas in your finances, prioritizing them with numbers.

   - I do not have a budget
   - I have no idea of how much I owe
   - Late fees are common in my household
   - I always run out of money before the next pay check
   - Large bills overwhelm my finances
   - Coupons, sales, and saving money are not a way of life for me
   - The credit card is at or close to the limit
   - I have no savings
   - Other:

   ____

   ____

2. Because I know He wants me to be free of the anxiety of debt and financial loss, my prayer for God's customized solution for my finances is as follows:

   ____

   ____

   ____

3. The Scripture that encourages me to organize my finances is the following:

____

____

____

(This is a good time to read and follow "It's Time to Organize Those Finances.")

4. In order to complete my prioritized tasks, I will need to do the following:
(Examples: create a budget, call the credit card company, and negotiate a lower interest rate or pay-off amount, begin to save money with every purchase, save for large yearly bills, put money into a savings/investment plan, etc.)

____

____

____

____

5. (*To be completed when a budget is written down and at least a month after beginning to follow your new, customized "financial plan."*)
I see that God helped me accomplish changing my finances for the better. My feelings about my finances now are (include today's date):

____

____

____

6. My *one year later* journal entry about my finances is the following (include the date):

____

____

____

It's Time to Organize Those
Finances

You will be learning *what to pay* and *when to pay* in this organizing project. Let's start with *what to pay* first. Here are some suggested tools: paper shredder, calculator, note pad or tablet, and your small file with current bill stubs. These should give you help during this all-important organizing job. You will only need the "Trash" and "Save" containers for this job.

A Budget

Isn't the word "budget" scary? I never had an accounting course yet found creating a *workable budget* to be easier than I thought. You just have to understand the difference between income and expenditures (bills/debt). It really is easier than you think! Let's look at those two items and break them down to be easily understood.

Income

Tablet ready? Write down what your *income is monthly.* If you and your spouse both work, it is the very best to live on only one income, but you may not be able to do this until you pay down current debt. For now, *write a total income that you are earning or comes in monthly.*

Keep this income figure at the top of your paper. Our example will be $4000.00. Please note that the amounts used in this illustration may be higher or lower than your figures and are not actual costs or income.

Bills/Needs/Expenditures

List those bills that come on a monthly basis. Here are some examples:

- House Payment/Rent: $633.00
- Electric: $60.00
- Gas/Heat: $115.00
- Cable TV/Satellite: $50.00
- Garbage: $12.00
- Car Payment: $438.00
- *Church (Tithe): $400.00*
- Subtotal: $1,708.00

Next you need to add to the list an approximate monthly budget for groceries and gas:

- Groceries: $320.00
- *Gas: $100.00*
- Subtotal: $2,128.00

Next, you will need to add how much it is costing you for items that are not necessarily billed on a monthly basis, but *overwhelm* your budget when you get the bills. *Please take note here:* we will take the total you are billed for a year and divide it by the twelve months to see how much you need to budget *monthly (save)* in advance to pay these large, yearly bills. Examples:

- Car Insurance: $2000.00 yearly
- Life Insurance: $1000.00 yearly
- Property Taxes: $3000.00 yearly
- Car License Plates: $200.00 yearly
- House Insurance: $900.00 yearly
- *Club Membership: $500.00 yearly*
- Subtotal: $7,600.00

Now, *divide the $7600 by 12 months* and you know you *need to save $633* per month in order to pay these bills.

Now let's get a *final budget.*

- Using the $2,128 (subtotal above of monthly bills plus groceries and gas)
- *Adding the $ 633 (needed to save monthly for yearly expenses*)
- Total = $2,761 is your current budget *need or expenditure*
- Remember that $4,000 *income* figure?
- *Deduct the $2,761 needs or expenditures figure from that.*
- Balance: $1,239 (in your "pocket") for miscellaneous

What Was Not Noted In the Example Budget

There was not a provision for *emergency needs* (i.e. car repairs, appliance breakdowns, etc.)

It was not shown *how to set aside* the monthly money for the large yearly expenditures. Perhaps I can help you start this by my own example:

PERSONAL ORGANIZING STORY

When we were first married, our finances were completely devastated about every three months by a car insurance bill. So I paid service fees for the privilege of making quarterly or monthly installments as this came due. Later, we began to need money for the yearly property taxes and house insurance. There just was no money for these expenses. Young, newly married, new babies in the home and college expenses to pay left us living on the edge of starvation every few months in order to scrape up enough money to meet these large bills.

I felt inadequate to find a solution to the problem.

I had no experience in budgeting or paying bills even though I was a pretty disciplined, thrifty person. I knew I needed help from a Power bigger than our paycheck, bigger than our bank. I began to pray for wisdom to create a "budget," a *plan* to keep money aside for these huge payments yet pay current bills. God answered me with one simple thought, "save." A plan began to formulate in my mind to save enough money to pay these bills as they came, but in the meantime, I had to pay the *current large expenses* as well. It took nearly two years to save enough to begin to write checks for these large, overwhelming amounts as they came due, but it created a *consistency* in our budget. We began to have "even" paychecks, not "peaks and valleys." I was still young but learned a wise, aged rule: God is interested in our money and He will guide and protect it... if we ask for His help. He gave a customized plan to answer my customized request!

The trick is to be saving *while still paying* the current year's large bills. Unless you can use some large income bonus or income tax refund to start this savings program, it will take you a while to get it going, too. However, it will be worth it! There will no longer be the stress of the huge bills coming in and no money to pay them. Be patient. Look at this as a long-term goal resulting from a long-term plan.

This money can be directly withdrawn and deposited monthly/weekly into a credit union or a bank savings account for future use. I personally keep this money in my checking account since the bills for these expenses come due all throughout the year. Since savings account interest is so low, it seems easier to just keep it in the checking account. I am not tempted to spend it. But this could be a very real problem for some. In that case, the money should be directly deposited into a separate account to be accessed as needed. Today's online and over-the-phone banking simplifies fund transfers from a savings account to a checking account.

If you are able to keep it in the checking account without temptation, try deducting and highlighting the amounts in a bright ink in your checkbook record. *Do not show this money in your current checkbook balance.* Keep a running total of the amounts being saved. Because this amount is always highlighted in a colored ink in your checkbook, it is easy to spot. Because you will always have this money in your checkbook, you will not run the risk of overdrawn checks or fees. You will have a "backup" in your account, but you need to be *disciplined* so that you do not spend any of it without replacing it.

Emergency Funds, Credit Cards

There are many financial advisors who will tell you that you need to have two or more months' salary on hand in case of hard times (unemployment), so much saved for emergencies, and never use credit cards. *I agree with them totally*. But the plain truth is that most Americans are just "getting by" and really don't have a plan or a method of saving. My goal in discussing organizing your office and your finances is to help you begin to *find the bills* and *pay on time.*

After you have created a *workable budget* and you can *file away documents* after paying the bills and actually *find them again*, it is time to discuss other features of finances that we really find hard to think about.

Get Out Of Debt

If you are unable to find a way to pay off bills, you may need some professional help. *By all means, see a financial advisor.* There are also some very good financial courses out there for Christians that teach God-honoring methods of clearing our debt and using our temporary resources for eternal purposes. Seek out those who have proven financial responsibility and take some of their advice. Ask for their recommendations for a local financial consultant. Whatever you do, *commit to getting out of debt* and not getting back into debt in the future. It will drain not only your purse, but your joy, your relationships, and perhaps even your ministries for the Lord.

May I share *my method* of clearing debt for over 40 years? Here it is:

- *Tithe* to the Lord.
- Never use a credit card for more than I can *pay within 1 month.*
- If I use credit cards, I use them to get the "cash back" or other rewards and *keep a zero balance* each month.
- Never agree to debt that is beyond my ability to pay ... *always being willing to "walk away."*
- *Keep bills paid each payday.*
- Use whatever means I can to *save:* coupons, sales, clearances, rebates, etc.
- If something is faulty and has a guarantee, apply it and *get new merchandise or a repair.* I can do this because I can find my guarantee and sales receipt.
- *Seek* good advice and *watch* what others do who handle their money wisely.

- *Conserve* in whatever area I can: gasoline, food, clothing, laundry products, restaurant meals, etc.

When to Pay Bills: On Time and Never Late

You can do a very quick analysis of this by figuring out your pay periods. Are you paid weekly, bi-weekly or monthly? At what time or dates of the month do the bills come due? Put these facts down on paper. Next, arrange them by date through the month. An example would be house payment, first of month, car payment due fifth of month, garbage bill due tenth of month, and so forth. Now, draw a line beneath those bills that come due in the *first half* of the month into that *combined income period,* no matter when you receive your pay. Put the bills that come due in the latter half of the month into that combined pay period. You really have only one amount of pay per month, no matter when you receive it. Looking at it in "halves" helps you visualize the overall budget and begin to live evenly, without the feast and famine routine.

Getting those bills paid on time can be assisted by using several convenient and accurate methods. Of course, you should already be using *direct deposit* for your income. Try using your banking institution's *electronic fund transfer* for as many payments as possible. This EFT can be used for one or several accounts. Many banks allow several electronic payments at no charge. Check it out locally.

Now you can begin holding money back on pay periods that do not have as many expenses for the pay periods that have more bills than pay. Does this make sense? Give it at least a three month try, adjusting it as needed to include those large, yearly expenses that sneak up and leave us breathless, out of cash and living in a famine every so often. In achieving this, you will begin to have your bills paid on time and uniformity in your finances.

Make a Plan for Your Future

It is not only good to save, but it is God-honoring to plan to care for ourselves. This can be done by ridding ourselves of debt and saving for future needs such as a car, health care, etc. The help of a financial advisor can be invaluable for retirement plans. Begin small, and think big!

Conclusion

There is so much that could be written about finances, but *my goal here is to help you organize your bill payment methods and your files and to get on the right track with your finances.* Real financial planning is a lifelong process and takes knowledge and commitment. You will find as you take the "baby steps" of creating a budget, paying bills on time, and finding important documents, that you are ready to branch out to savings and lifelong investment programs.

Give Credit to the Lord

When you have worked through your finances and budget, take time to praise and thank the Lord.

O God, my Provider, I praise and thank You for all You have given to me to more than meet my needs each day. I thank You for giving me the wisdom to work through creating a budget and for helping me figure out how I need to improve some of the uses of the money You provide. Please help me to learn to be generous with others as You have been so generous to me. Help me to let go of what I cannot keep. Help me to have an eternity view of money and "things." With Your help I will remain timely in these payments and bring honor to You by having a good and honest reputation. I thank and praise You for all Your blessings in my life. I pray in the name of Jesus. Amen.

Now go back a few pages and complete *My Financial Journal.*

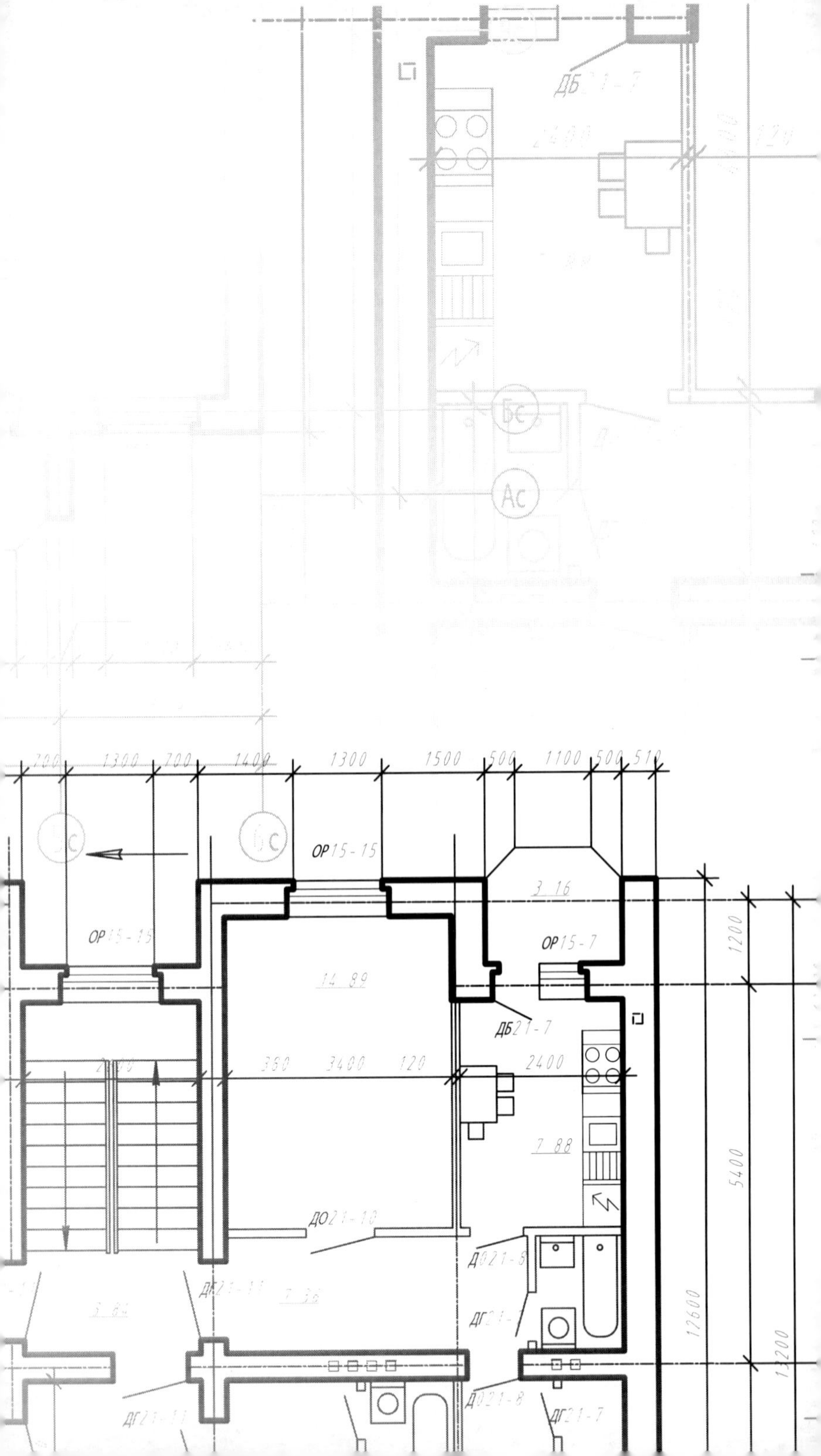

700
1300
700
1400
1300
1500
500
1100
500
510
ОР15-15
ОР15-15
3.16
ОР15-7
14.89
ДБ21-7
360
3400
120
2400
7.88
1200
5400
ДО21-10
ДО21-8
ДГ21-11
ДО21-8
ДГ21-7
12600
13200

Calendars, Clocks, and Other Useless Junk

Time Management

Remember the country song "I'm in a Hurry and I Don't Know Why?" The next line goes, "I rush and rush till the day I die." That could be written by about 98% of the American population. We try talking on our cell phones while we drive or shop so we don't have to sit down and have that conversation. We drive like we are going to the emergency room with a sick child; then we push and shove to get in the shortest lines at the supermarket, so we can get home to serve the take-out we bought because we don't have time to cook between meetings. I am out of breath just writing that!

Why do we feel we are always rushing, yet we are still behind? How can we solve this? Can we make some changes without smashing the clock, ripping up the calendar, crushing our PDA, or chaining ourselves to the bedpost? God wants us to have a different lifestyle. That is why He talks so much about rest in the Bible. Even Jesus, on numerous occasions, went off to be alone. Yes, He had busy times with large crowds, but then He took time to be alone, have a quieter setting. Do you think you need time apart from activity sometimes? Do you think you can change your schedule in order to feel less stressed? Do you think this would be pleasing to the Lord? Or do you think that He enjoys watching you chase around on your current schedule?

God is a God of busy and of quiet. He loves for you and me to accomplish a lot of work, but He loves it when we enjoy Him, enjoy our family, enjoy His creation, and enjoy other people. As we study His Word concerning "time management," let's seek His sound guidance to evaluate our priorities. We need to understand that it is not always *what* we are doing as much as *how* we are doing it. Through prayer, God can reveal to us the difference and help us make necessary changes. Let's go.

Dear Father, I feel in a hurry even as I pray. I am always in a hurry, yet feel I never can accomplish what is really important to me or You. Will You speak to me as I study these Bible verses and show me where I can change my schedules and habits? I want to create a life with less stress for my family and for myself. I know this will help my health, my moods, and my ability to focus on You. I ask You to bless the meditation of my heart on Your Word. I pray these things in the name of Jesus. Amen.

Feeling Beastly Yet Beautiful

Shampooing the Carpet

And let the favor of the Lord our God be upon us; and do confirm for us the work of our hands; Yes, confirm the work of our hands.

—Psalm 90:17

I had readied myself for the task ahead by making supper the day before and doing the morning cleaning tasks in record time. I had all the bedrooms straight and the family room vacuumed. It was early yet, so I decided to have my devotions before I ran to town to rent the carpet machine. Deciding on a portion of the Psalms, this verse stood out at me from the page and was my prayer that morning. Even though I was to be shampooing a dirty carpet, I prayed for the "favor (or beauty) of the Lord our God" to be upon me and show through me that day. And I also prayed for God to establish the work of my hands that I could glorify Him in whatever I did.

The young sales clerk helped me load the heavy, awkward shampoo unit and all the tools into the back of my truck. I arrived home, and it was still only ten o'clock. I would be done in fine time at this rate! I dragged the shampoo unit, or more truthfully, it dragged me into the house. Hooking everything together according to the instruction book, it seemed something was missing—the nozzle end of the hose that did the actual cleaning. I rushed to the phone and called the hardware store only to be greeted by the same young salesman. Yes, he had forgotten to give me one part, and would I check the shampoo he had given me? Upholstery shampoo! Back to the truck I flew and started the five mile trip back to town for my missing part and the correct shampoo. About three minutes later, I felt like I was boiling as I was muttering something about incompetence and youthful inexperience. I heard a little voice saying, "You can handle this two ways. You can go in and give him a piece of your over-heated mind mentioning gasoline prices and your precious time or you can 'let the favor (beauty) of the Lord our God be upon you.'" Sheepishly, I decided I had a great opportunity here to witness through attitude to this boy. Asking the Lord to please shine through me, I entered the store and smilingly took my new supplies and left with a thank you.

That carpet had never looked cleaner and was still done in record time. I am sure the Lord did establish the work of my hands that day. Here is a real incentive for a housewife to be obedient to the Lord. Where else could we get a sure promise for "beauty" *and* efficient work?

O dear God, I give You the work of my hands for this day. Bless this work that I am about to do, and may it bring praise to You. May my house reflect You; may my life reflect You. Remind me in all that I do that You bring the blessing for work well done. Thank You for that. Amen.

Stranded

Errands

Let your character be free from the love of money, being content with what you have; for He Himself has said, "I will never desert you, nor will I ever forsake you."

—Hebrews 13:5

It was a busy day, as every wash day is. Except this day I had to go to vote in the local school elections, too. Having finished my last load of clothes, I jumped in the truck to run this errand.

Before I reached the school where we vote, I noticed a small amount of steam coming from the side of the hood when I stopped at an intersection. When I arrived at the school, I found water spewing out the bottom of the truck near the radiator. *Overheated,* I thought. It only took a few minutes to vote. Turning the key back on, I saw the temperature gauge was reading about 190°. Something must be wrong. I decided to drive the two blocks to my husband's job and trade for the car, letting him, the "master mechanic," take it to the garage for a checkup. Well, he was gone and would not be back for at least another hour.

It was all up to me now. Maybe I could make it home if I drove slowly. No, the temperature was over 200° within two blocks. I inched to the nearest gas station and turned off my now pressure-cooker-looking truck. The attendant took one look and surmised that I had a broken heater hose. An elderly gentleman standing nearby tried to console me by telling me how helpless women were in mechanical emergencies and how little we actually knew about motors. He kept smiling and nodding to himself, and I was certain he was thoroughly enjoying my whole frustrating situation.

After he trimmed and clamped the hose, the mechanic was sure I could make it home. Turning the motor on, he refilled the radiator with water only to find it spurting out on the ground as fast as he poured it. The hose had a complete tear and needed replacing, not mending.

Needless to say, the truck was fixed, and I was able to return home—about two hours later, but home. The truck failed me, leaving me without transportation, my husband was gone when I needed him, and the mechanic did not fix the hose correctly until the second try. How thankful I am that the Lord never leaves us in time of need or trial. He promises to never forsake us, and He cannot lie.

Do you feel stranded, alone? Does the "truck" of your life seem to be breaking down all the time and no one seems to be able to fix it? Call on God to make His presence known to you. His promise is true. Only man can leave you stranded and alone—never God.

My dear Heavenly Father, thank You for Your promise to never leave me or forsake me. O God, what assurance that brings to my life. What peace I claim because of this promise. You are so good to me. Thank You for loving me and standing by me, no matter what. I love You. I pray this because of Jesus. Amen.

"God is patient with the process! *Think of the* enormous leisure *of God! He is* never *in a hurry."*

Oswald Chambers

The Waiting Game
Patience

The Lord is good to those who wait for Him, to the person who seeks Him, It is good that he waits silently for the salvation of the Lord.

—Lamentations 3:25–26

Rest in the Lord and wait patiently for Him ...

—Psalm 37:7a

Waiting seems to be the woman's game in life. We wait a lot! We wait in the doctor's office with sick kids. We wait for piano and music lessons. We wait for soccer practice, football practice, and every other sport that can be practiced. We wait in the longest grocery lines because our carts never have ten items or less. We wait for everyone to come home when a meal is ready only to keep waiting just a little longer. We wait with a car full of kids while hubby gets just "one" item at the hardware store. Yes, sometimes I even have to wait to use the bathroom. We probably do more waiting in a lifetime than our male counterparts.

Do you ever get sick of waiting? Do you think there has to be something more productive to do with these hours than to be just sitting and waiting?

Christ waited. He waited thirty years to begin His ministry. He waited until His testing was over in the wilderness. He waited all night in the garden of Gethsemane for His Father to make His will known to Him. He waited long, torturous hours on the cross for you and for me to complete His magnificent gift for us. Now, He is waiting in heaven for us to welcome us home.

How can I feel so pompous to say that I have waited at all when I see how He has waited to provide me with forgiveness, redemption, and eternal life? Can I give Him a few minutes of my day, my week, my life? Can I not "wait one hour" with Him? Oh, that we may be good "waiters" as He was and is.

Dear Father, forgive my impatient lifestyle. Please forgive my complaining attitude. Please give me the gift of endurance. Help me to be patient with life itself. Remind me today of Christ sitting in heaven, waiting for me to enter and join Him there. Amen.

Creaking Doors and Squeaking Hinges

Pressure/Stress

Now He who establishes us with you in Christ and anointed us is God.

—II Corinthians 1:21

Torture experts admit that constant creaks and squeaks can wear a person's nerves to the breaking limits. And it seems that every house has one area that develops this nerve-shattering, teeth-grinding noise that is relentless.

Our torturous squeak was located, of all places, in the piano. It is painful enough to pay for three music lessons and doubly painful to listen to three lessons being practiced daily. But the pain of listening to a squeaking piano is beyond endurance. One day, I could stand it no more! Grabbing the oil can, I attacked the piano. Oil on each pedal. *Squeak, squeak.* I pulled off the lower front panel and oiled every moving part in sight. *Squeak, squeak.* Lying on the floor with my oil can in hand, I ordered my daughter to play. She sensed her mother was on the edge of insanity when I stuck my head up into the piano cavity. I found it! *Squirt. Squirt.* I watched as the oil oozed down the pedal controls from high above. As the oil was worked through the controls with each push of the pedal, the squeak grew fainter until it disappeared completely. Victory at last!

What causes squeaks and creaks in our homes? Sometimes moving parts are too tightly fitted, putting stress on the point where they meet creating noises. You would shout too if something was pinching you or trying to squeeze you. A lubricant, such as oil, relieves the pressure and makes both parts slide past one another.

Life itself puts a lot of pressure on all of us. We have financial pressures, job pressures, parenting pressures, marriage pressures, and spiritual pressures. We squeak and creak and moan under those pressures. From God's Word, we find that we have an unction, an anointing, or a lubricant from God. This unction or lubricant frees us from pressure; it moves us easily through life, relieving us, comforting us. Simply by inviting Christ to be our personal Savior, we receive this anointing, this balm for our souls. It comes in the form of the Holy Spirit. Through daily prayer, daily meditating on the Word, this Holy Spirit comes to glide us through one more day.

Find the squeakiest hinge or the creakiest door in your house. Go oil it up and listen; quietness. Remember your oil, your balm, your anointing from God the Father and thank Him for supplying His Holy Spirit in your life.

My dear Heavenly Father, I feel the pressures of my life squeezing me. Please cover me with Your Holy Spirit. Anoint me, and make me to "glide" between and through these pressures as You direct my path. Remind me that You are the balm I need for my spirit. Thank You, Father. Amen.

"At the end of your life, you will never regret not having passed one more test, not winning one more verdict or not closing one more deal. You will regret time not spent with a husband, a friend, a child, or a parent."

Barbara Bush, First Lady 1989–1993

My Time Management Journal

"I promise to work on my schedule, routines, and meal preparations and not take on the organization of any other room until I feel my pace and our family lifestyle are less stressed and in a better order."

1. Circle or name three major problems in your time management, prioritizing them with numbers.

    - I have no family "calendar"
    - I am embarrassed to have people know the chaos of my lifestyle
    - I am frequently late or miss appointments
    - Family meals are rare
    - When my family is at home, I frequently use fast food to save time
    - I have no schedule or routine for laundry, cleaning or meal preparation
    - I work away from the home many hours a week
    - I volunteer for several positions
    - I feel unable to keep up with my family's activities
    - I'm always in a hurry, yet never "caught up"
    - I am a single woman/mom and have little to no help
    - I feel there is a lot of stress in my home because of my family's "pace"
    - Other:

____

____

2. Because I know He created time and wants me to live with less stress, my prayer for God's customized plan for managing my time is the following:

___

___

___

3. The Scripture that encourages me to get control of my schedule and work habits is the following:

___

___

___

4. In order to complete my prioritized tasks, the helps that I will have to assemble will be:

___

___

___

___

(This is a good time to read and follow "It's Time to Organize That Time Management.")

5. *(To be completed 2–6 weeks after working with a new routine/schedule)*
   I see that God has great plans for my time and our time as a family. My feelings about my schedule and our family routines are as follows (include today's date):

___

___

6. My *one year later* journal entry about my schedule and my family's lifestyle/pace is the following (include the date):

It's Time to Organize That

Time Management

This will undoubtedly be a monumental task. The answers are multiple and not so simple. *But there is hope.* Like organizing a room, find a place in your life to start *evaluating* and *making changes.*

Why is it we feel we are always in a hurry?

Why can't we make it to any event on time?

Why can't we get more out of our twenty-four hours like our friends?

Why can't we ever have a meal ready for our family?

Why? Why? Why?

A whole book could be written (and many of them have been) on time management instead of just a short section like this one. The questions above and many more indicate that we are running in the same circle as the rest of the world, trying to get twenty-eight hours of work and fun out of every twenty-four hours. Where can we get off this merry-go-round? How do we do it? Do we need to stop everything that we are doing in order to slow our lives down? Do we need to quit our jobs and stop helping at our children's school in order to have a "decent" meal on the table each day? How can we remain "super moms" and give up anything?

Finding a Place to Start

Begin your evaluation process with your calendar in hand. What does your next week look like? What does your next month look like? What will be the changes or additions with the next season? Examples would be sport schedules, summer break, work vacation, yard work/landscaping, etc. How will these additions impact the family routines or time together? How many nights are you gone to meetings or other events? If needed, write down answers to these questions. You will begin to see patterns or "overload" if they are there.

Always keep a planner or purse calendar (or PDA) and *a family calendar at home* so they can be kept synchronized. As you make appointments away from the house, record it on your purse calendar. Transfer this information to the family calendar when returning home. I suggest month-at-a-glance calendars so you can have an overall picture of the schedules of the family. This will give you a tool in evaluating if you have too many activities in one week of the month or on any particular day, so you can prepare meals accordingly, plan the use of your cars, plan child care, and so forth. The calendar will be your best helper in making changes in your time commitments.

A suggestion for a family calendar: Visit your local office supply store, and get one of the wall-size, dry-erase calendars. Enter each individual's schedule in a different color ink. This will make each separate activity stand out.

When evaluating changes in your time management, you must first of all consider balance and guarded control. These will incorporate not only *what* you are doing, but *how* you are doing it.

Balance

Sometimes, like a good tree, we just need to "prune" the activity, not cut it down. Change the way it is growing in your life. Step back, see the big picture, and decide where we are out of control. Is one area lopsided, and you wanted to spend time in other ways? Make a written list, one to ten, of your priorities for activities. Follow this with a list, one to ten, of your current activities. Do they match? Pray over them. Seek wisdom and discernment. Then, begin making decisions that will lead you to take *guarded control.*

Guarded Control

Guarded control means *limiting* the amount of your life you are willing to let each activity occupy. After your prayerful evaluation, you will be able to make changes or prune those areas you want to lessen and *guard* those areas of value to you. The word "no" will become valuable and freeing to you.

Because we cannot buy a shelving unit or storage bins to solve our time management problems, let's begin by considering situations and scenarios. Which one fits you or your lifestyle? You may want to take these in a different order than offered, but please consider each point. After looking at these scenarios, there will be suggested *solutions.*

Career Woman Scenario

Before we begin evaluating different problems that face a career woman, let's evaluate the work itself. Here are some very real questions to ask about your job:

- Do you really *need* to work outside the home?
- If you did not work outside the home, would you have enough income to support the *necessities of your household?*
- If you did not work, how much money would be saved on car, gas, clothing, food, and child care that you now spend to support your working?

- If you remain working, would changing to *fewer hours or different hours* enable you to have less stress and keep things in better condition at home?
- Make a definite evaluation whether you are working to provide *necessities* or a *lifestyle.*

A PERSONAL ORGANIZING STORY

I had a wonderful, young client who really needed to work to supplement her husband's income. She was working three hours a day, five days a week. She was having trouble getting supper on the table each day, paying for child care, and laundry was seldom completed and put away. She was working very hard at home and on her job, yet she was feeling—and actually was—always behind. As her organizer, the easiest solution would have been to suggest that she quit her job or reduce her hours. But, I knew this would effect the family income. I began to ask God to show me changes she could make while doing no harm to her earnings. God answered by giving me a good look at my own working hours. I was working a "flexible" schedule at the time. This allowed me to get my office work done, earn what I needed yet still be able to help my organizing clients. Could this work for her?

We looked at her job and hours first of all. Her position did not require her to be in the office every day either, yet she had about fifteen hours of work to do. She approached her employer, and he agreed to let her come into the office two days a week for six hours and to also do some work at home. She now had the flexibility to prepare extra meals ahead of time, complete laundry, and spend more time with her children on the days she was not in the office. Life became less stressful, she was happier, her family profited by having good meals and family time in the evening. Her earnings did not change. She actually realized more money because she had cut down on clothing requirements for the office and wasted money on child care and take-out food. The *change* in hours, not the *elimination* of hours, made all the difference. That's such a picture of what God wants us to do every day: change, be flexible. Life is always changing and we should be, too. He proved again that He is interested in our time, our earnings, our requests for help.

Could This Work for You?

Whether away from the home for a full-time or part-time job, you are still away from the home significant amounts of time each day, each week. Let's *evaluate* the facts:

- You cannot keep an absolutely clean home and be gone to a job.
- You cannot be cooking dinner while at your job.
- You cannot serve on very many volunteer positions when you work outside the home.
- Your family is just as important to you as that of a stay-at-home wife or mother.
- Your desires for your family are just the same as the desires of a stay-at-home woman.

Suggested Solutions

Now that you have been realistic about the position you are in, let's evaluate some *options:*

- Ask yourself, "Could a part-time housekeeping person help me feel in control of the cleanliness of my home?" This could be a person who does *only* all the "extra" duties for you, like cleaning the grout in the showers, dusting above windows and doorways, washing and dusting knick-knacks, etc.

- Try preparing multiple meals at a time and freezing some for future use. This could be done on weekends or by using a crock pot and oven meal one day to prepare two to three days' worth of meals.
- *Try the word "no"* or express the need for time to evaluate the request when asked to take on new time commitments. Remember, you were hired for a specific job. Why do they now want you to do more? Perhaps a good question for your employer would be, "You hired me to do X, Y, and Z. Which one of these tasks would you like me to set aside in order to do this additional task?" This is not impertinent or disrespectful. Be firm.
- The time spent at home must *incorporate the family* while they are there. The supper meal and evening should be spent for the most part as a family unit since you are so detached all day. This will take great *commitment by all family members* to make it work.
- Keep *goals* in mind as you schedule on your calendar. If family time is your goal, every evening cannot be booked with events.

Stay-at-Home Woman Scenario

You do realize that you are the "Volunteer Queen" and that your name tops the list when someone needs help, don't you? The prior scenario fits you except that you do not get paid. You are not gone eight to ten hours a day, but your other activities and volunteer positions pull you away from home and add to your workload. You need to do some evaluating:

- Are you too busy?
- Are you accomplishing what you hoped to as a stay-at-home woman/mom/wife?
- Is your family gathering for a meal or game daily?
- Have you discussed family direction and priorities with your spouse?

Suggested Solutions

Many stay-at-home women have worse schedules and communicate with spouses and children less than career women because they do not have their priorities in view. They are deriving a lot of recognition from their volunteer positions. They are busy keeping busy, so everyone notices how busy they are!

If you are a married, stay-at-home woman, discuss priorities and goals with your husband first and foremost. Ask him if your home-life is what he hoped for by sacrificing your income to stay at home. If it is not, discuss how you can work together to make it more of a reality.

If asked to expand or take on a new volunteer position, use the word "no" or the phrase "I really need to evaluate if I can do more." You took on a volunteer position for a specific duty. Why do they want you to do more now? *Be firm.* (See *Career Woman Suggested Solutions.*)

Balance and guarded control need to be your *guidelines* and also your *goals.*

Mother of Sports-Minded Teens Scenario

Another Personal Example

Every mother, working or stay-at-home, hits a new "plateau" when the children enter sports. We had three high school teenagers at one time and lived about five miles from town. They all wanted to be active in sports, but we *limited* their involvement to one sport per child per school year. That way the entire family could enjoy watching them play, we were on the road a little less, and they had time to commit to their studies, church, and family. These decisions were carefully thought about and discussed by us as parents and fit some goals we had for our family. With a hectic sports calendar, we could not book something every evening and have time to be together.

While I realize this is not a popular decision in our sports-minded society, my husband and I felt that our priority was to maintain a strong family unit while our children were in the home. We felt we could not accomplish that or have good family communications if we were on the road or gone every evening. We believe it truly is *quantity time* that leads to good discussions and shows an investment in children's lives. "Quantity time" is a leading factor in "quality time."

We always wanted to spend at least one meal at the table together with our children each day. Supper was an easy choice when they were younger. However, as our children got to their later teens, while participating in sports, that meal became breakfast. Breakfast was fun, talkative, and binding as they went off to school. There were lots of discussions on things happening at school, friends, sports. We did not have as much "quantity time," but our priorities were still accomplished by taking action to reach our goals.

Suggested Solutions:

- Discuss your goals together as parents for the time you want to spend as a family.
- Discuss these goals with the children and *respectfully consider their desires* for participation in sports or other activities.
- *Look for a balance.* Some weeks or seasons may be a bit more hectic than others, but look at the big picture: the overall time together must be guarded.
- Try to have one gathering per day. After looking at all schedules, start making any changes to accomplish your goals.

Single Woman/Mother Scenario

Need we say you *must* work outside the home? If you have children, you are trying to do the jobs of both mother and father. Since you are single, your name is always second on the list for volunteers, after the married-stay-at-home moms. You carry the entire burden of all housekeeping, cooking, shopping, finances, and possibly home maintenance and yard work as well. You are even more stretched than the rest of us. How can you do it all?

Looking back to the previous scenarios, you see that *evaluation* is the first step in finding control of your schedule. Consider these issues in your life:

- What are the hours I must work?
- How much time do I have at home?
- Is my job flexible enough to change any hours and not lose pay?
- Do I have any talents I cannot pursue because I am too busy?

- If you are a mother, what jobs can your children do to help?
- *And this is the "Every Woman" question: Do I ever have any "me" time?*

Suggested Solutions:

- Pursue slight changes in work schedules to free up more time. Example: Instead of five, eight-hour days, can you work four, ten-hour days?
- Is it possible to *trade talents or work* with someone in order to be more efficient at home? Example: You like to cook so you would make three extra meals (as you are cooking your own) per week in exchange for someone who could mow your lawn or do basic cleaning weekly.
- If you are a mother, try training even young children how to change their beds, pick up toys, dust furniture, bring their dirty dishes to the sink, hang up clothing, etc. With older children, you could establish a routine schedule for them to help with vacuuming, basic cleaning chores, laundry, and even cooking.
- After evaluating work requirements or volunteer positions, remember again that you were hired or volunteered for a *specific* job. Why are they asking for you to do more? (See the *Career Woman Suggested Solutions.*) Realistically, they know your forty hours are already full. Your responsibility is to fulfill what you were hired for and then to take care of yourself and your family. You cannot keep yourself healthy or happy by working longer and harder at your job. *Be firm in these commitments.*
- The "me" time can only be found one way: *You*

really must schedule it in order to get it. Whether it is time at the gym, time to sew, to read or to garden, determine which day or days you can set time aside just to be you. This time will refresh and reward you with a feeling of satisfaction plus control.

Conclusion

Women's roles are as varied as our hairdos! Isn't that great? We do not all fit the same mold, but God has planned it that way. Whether single, married, with children, without children, your time or schedules can only be controlled by you. You hold the strings to the decisions about every minute of every day. Take steps to begin to rein in those activities that you have *evaluated* as out of control. Take steps to begin to enjoy your days by creating and enforcing a *new plan of action.* Remember, balance and guarded control need to be our guidelines and also our goals.

Give Credit to the Lord

Dear Creator of all life, I realize You created the twenty-four hours called a day and You seek to be Lord of my time and how I use it. Please bless my mind with the ability to find a balance in my activities and the strength to continue to guard my time and energy to be used wisely for You.

I recognize every day is a gift from You and that I need to share this gift with my family and community. Help me see the shortness of my life and how each day and each activity is important to You. I give You my time, Lord. Amen.

Now go back a few pages and complete *My Time Management Journal.*

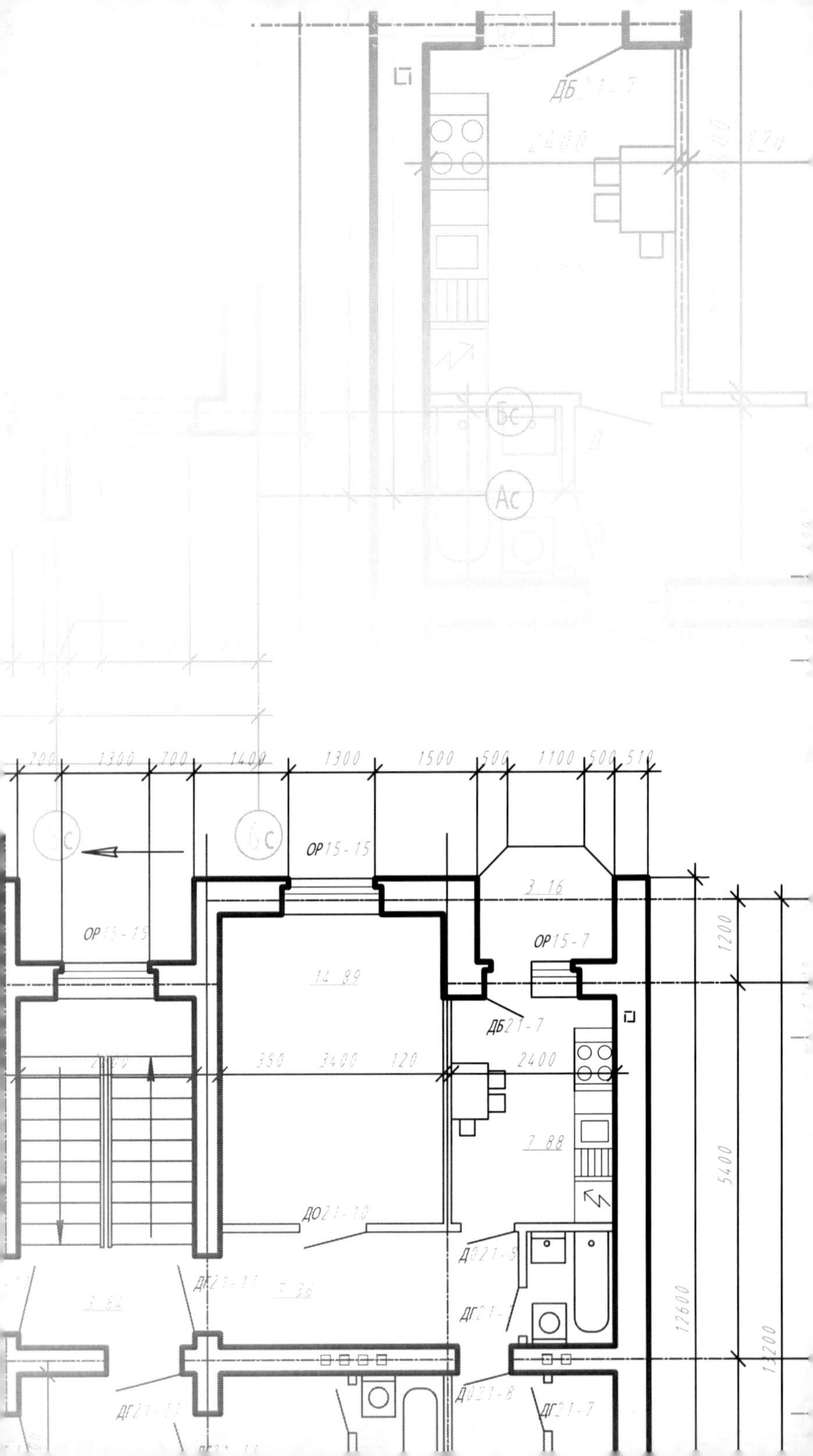

ДБ21-7
2400
Бс
Ас
700
1300
700
1400
1300
1500
500
1100
500
510
Бс
ОР15-15
ОР15-15
3.16
ОР15-7
14.89
1200
ДБ21-7
380
3400
120
2400
7.88
5400
ДО21-10
ДО21-8
ДГ21-11
ДГ21-7
12600
13200
ДГ21-11
ДО21-8
ДГ21-7

Up, Down, and All Around

The Attic/Basement/Seasonal Storage

Almost all of those rental storage units in our area have either the description "mini storage" or "affordable storage." Aren't those both oxymorons? If you need extra space to store your household overflow, do you really want something "mini"? I vote for *huge!* And affordable? How can paying for air and floor space be a good investment?

Every season and holiday, there is the dilemma of where to store seasonal decorations, camping gear, vulnerable deck or outdoor cushions, seldom used small appliances, and possibly even family heirlooms. Before we rent a unit to hold all of our extra stuff, we need to evaluate our attic or basement and the quantity of items to be stored.

So, let's turn our thinking to *minimal yet enjoyable*

items to store as well as the proper containers for storage. Evaluate the climate, and then evaluate the storage area(s) to be used. This will be a rewarding task as we sort through the Christmas decorations our children made, recall the scent of hot cider spiced with cinnamon sticks, launder suntan oils from the beach towels, and safely pack up those sparklers. No mice or mold are welcome in the reminders of joyful holidays and vacations.

God created these seasons for our enjoyment. Through watching those changes, He demonstrates His power as well as reminding us that our lives are always in transition. The enjoyment of all seasons can be enhanced as we properly store and then find what we need as those seasons change.

Dear precious Father, this task seems too hard. I will be pulling out all the things that I think are treasures. I am praying for discernment. Help me to find a way to keep those items that will create memories and to be strong in discarding those that I really do not need. Help me to find the right storage areas to preserve these things. I know that nothing is too hard for You, so make me like You: strong. Help me to have a good sense of humor about this difficult job. I pray in Your Name. Amen.

Bionic Christmas Trees

Holiday Storage

But whenever a man turns to the Lord, the veil is taken away. Now the Lord is the Spirit; and where the Spirit of the Lord is, there is liberty. But we all, with unveiled face beholding as in a mirror the glory of the Lord, are being transformed *into the same image from glory to glory, just as from the Lord, the Spirit.*

—II Corinthians 3: 16–18

Not everyone has the privilege of growing Christmas trees to sell. Taking the old trailer out to the trees, we would inspect each one for uniformity before cutting them. A straight top branch was required on each one to hold that star or angel. Of course, not every one was perfect, but beauty is in the eye of the beholder … right? Customer after customer came. Little children ran around trying to select their perfect tree while chattering about the decorations they made to put on it. Happily, they all carried home their Christmas trees stuffed into the trunks of their cars with the tops seeming to wave goodbye to us as they drove off.

As the Christmas trees were sold, only the "rejects" were left. They had branches missing here and there or were in some way imperfect. Of these left unsold, we got to choose *our* Christmas tree. We couldn't just burn them or throw them away!

Every year it was the Challenge of the Christmas Tree. It became my job to be the tree repair person since I had devised so many ways to do this. Handy with a drill, I'd dive into those bare spots between branches making a hole in the trunk. Into that hole, I would insert a branch that had either been pruned from the over-grown bottom or had broken off another ill-fated tree. To hold this "prosthetic branch" in place, I carefully wove a hammock-like sling from my husband's fishing line. Weaving it back and forth, up and down, it would become suspended from other sturdy branches. After adding several of these branches around the tree, it was ready to decorate. One had to be careful not to put too many lights or heavy ornaments on these precarious branches or they might collapse. As the last decoration, we always added silver aluminum icicles. No one ever guessed that we actually had transformed the homeliest, barest tree in the lot into our beautiful, shimmering Christmas tree.

Do you ever consider the transformation Christ wants to do for you or has already done for you? He takes us with broken dreams, broken lives and emptiness in our spirit. He weaves a support under us. He attaches that support to Himself and holds it firmly. He becomes a light in our lives. He begins to decorate our lives with the ornaments of love, joy, peace, patience, kindness, goodness, faithfulness, gentleness and self-control. These are all ornaments He intends for us to show others. He decorates us with Himself.

As you store those Christmas tree trimmings for another year, look at the sparkle and shine in each one. They are true reminders that even the homeliest, lowliest being can be made to glow because of Christ's great gift of love: the gift of eternal life.

Dear Lord, thank You that we will not be cast out or burned as those rejected trees for we have this new, transformed life in You. Thank You for a season that truly reminds us in every way of Your greatest gift to us: eternity with You. I pray in Your name. Amen.

"A word of kindness is seldom spoken in vain, while witty sayings are as easily lost as the pearls slipping from a broken string."[9]

George Prentice

Ring-Toss Tree Decorating

Holiday Storage

Anxiety in the heart of a man weighs it down. But a good word makes it glad.

— Proverbs 12:25

My mother-in-law would have been the first to admit that any type of decorating was not her gift. But accepting the poorest decorating efforts by someone else and neither laughing nor complaining at any shortcomings was definitely a commendable character trait. This was tested to the max each Christmas as Dad dragged in the yearly tree.

We never could understand why every year my father-in-law would select Christmas trees measuring only two to three feet tall. Their needles were so thin they looked like one of those hair-loss commercials. With only a few spindly branches, there really wasn't much to decorate. What we couldn't figure out was how he found trees this bad year after year. Was it a trick? Was it really the same pitiful fake tree? Or was it a ploy to get Mother to take over that job?

As Mother ran her restaurant, the job of decorating those little Charley Brown Christmas trees fell on Dad's shoulders. With only one string of large outdoor light bulbs, it was not a lengthy job. They hung down sadly, nearly breaking the thin branches with their weight. Next, he proudly hung the six or seven ornaments all on one side of the tree. As the tree drooped even more and tilted, he seemed to have struck upon the solution to balance it by simply tossing a long strand of heavy colored beads into the top and the other side. We thought he accomplished this by turning his back and giving a huge toss with all his might, landing those beads somewhere near the top, but still attached to the tree. Somehow, the tree remained upright, lit up, and it said "Merry Christmas."

Anxiety, like overweight and unevenly distributed tree decorations can unbalance our lives. It comes in so many forms that we hardly realize we are adding more and more pressure on ourselves. Perhaps you are already anxious about finances, and then your car breaks down. You become anxious about your job as you hear about lay-offs. Your anxiety about your health rises when you find a lump or a mole or a test reveals abnormalities. Because life is full of unknown twists and turns, anxiety becomes a part of it.

God wants us to *hear* a "good word." The best word to hear is God's Word. Open that Bible, and find reassurance that God is still in control of the entire universe and He certainly cares about your problems.

Then, *receive* a "good word" from a friend. How that encourages us when we know someone cares. Next, *spread* a "good word" by coming alongside someone you know who is anxious and going through a rough trial. Your "good word" can show God's love. God has chosen us to decorate this frail, unbalanced world. Hang your light, your ornament of love, on someone who needs to find balance and God's joy.

Dear Lord, help me to keep balance in my life by rejecting anxious feelings and thoughts. I know that helping others will keep my eyes off my own problems. Help me to be a light, an ornament and to speak a "good word" for You today. I am praying in Jesus' name. Amen.

The Scream Heard 'Round the Great Lakes

Seasonal Storage

And if it is disagreeable in your sight to serve the Lord, choose for yourselves today whom you will serve: whether the gods which your fathers served which were beyond the River, or the gods of the Amorites in whose land you are living; but as for me and my house, we will serve the Lord.

—Joshua 24:15

To be a twelve-year-old girl is tough enough, but to be that girl sandwiched between two brothers for the rest of your life is cruel and unusual punishment. Camping trips and confined quarters always made this point very clear. Each year our family would take a camping trip to a new destination and explore the wonders of nature and America. This was no luxury camping experience since we used our rusty farm truck equipped with a well-worn pick-up camper. It was not pretty, but it was serviceable, affordable, and fun.

The year we camped near the Mackinac Bridge was a bit chilly, as are a lot of Northern Michigan summers. Warm days and cool evenings made it easier to sleep five people foot to face in that tiny unit. When it rained, we just crammed inside and played card games, the kids told knock-knock jokes or read books, comic and otherwise. Unlike the huge RVs, which were big enough to have their own zip codes, that little camper had everything we needed with the exception of a bathroom. Walking over to the public restroom was an easy jaunt except during the night or in cases of emergencies.

One particular day, we were in the middle of a hot game of Crazy-eights, and we girls were winning. There was no time for a break, or we would have to forfeit. As the last card went down, our squirming daughter jumped up and ran out the door yelling, "I'll be back. I'm going to the restroom." Sadly accepting defeat, the guys all decided they might as well take a walk down to the restroom as well. Sauntering into the men's bathroom, my husband ran right into our daughter leaving it. "Wait a minute," he said. "What are you doing in here?" She looked at him, looked back at the bathroom, and then began screaming, "Ah-h-h-h-h-h!" The whole campground probably thought it was an air raid siren, but no, it was our beet-red, embarrassed daughter. As soon as we got her to unlock the camper door, she vowed never to be seen in public again. To calm her down, her two brothers laughed at her and poked fun for days showing her signs marked "men's" and "women's" and pointing out the difference. Her embarrassment was deep, but after a while, she was able to laugh at herself, and it has been a fun family memory ever since.

Choices. We make them all day, every day. Some are so easy, some are so difficult. As a wife and homemaker, I can choose to be dissatisfied with what I have and want more, more of everything. Would better furniture, a nicer home, a newer car, that huge RV, or better clothes be so bad? Or would being content with what God has provided for me be better? When it comes right down to it, *everything in life is a choice.* The really important choices are the ones that will last for eternity. What we do with our finances, our talents, our time, our minds will all have some eternal value if we choose to use them for eternal purposes.

Have you decided which door you will walk through? Do you feel desperate and afraid of making the wrong decision? Are you overshadowed by something large and looming resembling that huge RV? Like those bathroom doors, sometimes we can mistakenly choose to enter the wrong place or make the wrong decisions. Are we basing our decisions on a full view of the signs, or are we quickly running through life, hoping we get it right? I'm afraid many of us are just like that hurried little girl who ran full steam ahead, found something that met her needs, but left embarrassed and sorry for that quick decision.

In order to make the right decision and walk through the right door, we must first decide who we will follow. Like Joshua, make that decision today to follow only the Lord in all of your life decisions. Choosing God's way will always open the right door.

Dear God, I am looking for direction in making the right choices. I am choosing to follow You and to try to lead my entire family in following You. I know that this will bring peace to me, and I will never be embarrassed when I meet You. Please strengthen me today. Amen.

"Now is no time to think of what you do not have,
think of what you can do with what there is."

Ernest Hemingway

Easter Bunny Birthday

The Basement

And Jabez was more honorable than his brothers, and his mother named him Jabez saying "Because I bore him with pain." Now Jabez called on the God of Israel, saying, "Oh that thou wouldst bless me indeed, and enlarge my border, and that thy hand might be with me and that thou wouldst keep me from harm, that it may not pain me!" And God granted him what he requested.

—I Chronicles 4: 9–10

Every child deserves a memorable birthday party in his or her lifetime. Such was to be our daughter's fifth birthday. Born near the end of April, she could have been called a "Spring Baby." Often, the weather was balmy on her birthday.

With expectancy, I planned her little party. Can you believe her birthday fell on Easter weekend that year? What fun! We would have a big Easter egg hunt with all her little friends. We colored dozens of eggs. (Did I tell you eggs are cheap at Easter time?) Doing that job with a seven-, a five-, and a three-year-old should have been my first clue, but I'm a slow learner.

We invited her church class of ten children and some of her friends, making a total of about fifteen children who would be there. She was so excited. I readied the little house we were living in at the time. With a nine by twelve foot living room and only one bedroom on the main floor, it seemed a bit cramped for a party. But being outdoors for games of tag, red-rover, and the Easter egg hunt would help keep them busy in our large yard. The cake and decorations were all ready the night ahead of the big day.

Happy birthday! But we awoke to a white, Michigan

surprise the next morning. The yard, our cars, our trees were all covered with about three inches of wet snow. As the children began arriving for the two-hour party, I wondered how I would keep them busy for that long indoors. I hid all of the eggs in the living room while the children were in the bedroom. Fifteen excited, screaming children burst out and found the dozens of eggs in less than five minutes. I was sure my watch had stopped. No, only one hour and fifty minutes left. As I sat, dazed, the children lost direction and began chasing each other, trying to see who could get the most eggs. To say they were making egg salad would be mild.

If I just had a basement or a family room or somewhere to send these kids or gather them to play games. Instead of a basement, we had three cinder block walls and snow blowing in where the fourth one should have been. The day was saved with cake, candles, presents, and stories. Never in my life have I hated snow more than that day.

Space. More space. We all wish for and think we need more space. Our walls are boundaries, borders. We want more space between those walls. We think bigger is better.

In our spiritual life, can bigger be better? Can asking God for more, for larger boundaries be unselfish? If we are asking to be blessed and be a blessing to others, there is no selfishness involved. To quote Bruce Wilkinson in *The Prayer of Jabez*,

> When we ask for God's blessing, we're not asking for more of what we could get for ourselves. We're crying out for the wonderful, unlimited goodness that only God has the power to know about or give to us.[10]

Perhaps asking to have more space, a larger home, a larger yard, a finished, useable basement is selfish. But seeking an enlargement of our own usefulness for God's purposes is not. Do you want this "larger life"? Do you want to be a blessing to others by sharing God's truth? Do you desire to be blessed with the strength to resist sin or evil in your own life? Try asking God to "enlarge your territory," your spiritual boundaries. Just like Jabez, you will get a reply from God Himself.

Dear Lord, I want to have that large life. I want to be blessed by You with strength. I want to be a blessing to others. I have the faith to believe You hear and answer my prayers. Show me directly today Your blessing on my life. Amen.

My Attic/Basement/Seasonal Storage Journal

"I promise to work on these rooms and not take on the organization of any other room until my attic, basement, and seasonal storage are all in proper order."

1. Circle or name three problem areas in your attic or basement or seasonal storage areas, prioritizing them with numbers.

   - Items are not grouped by seasons
   - Items are not labeled
   - Seasonal items are difficult to access or reach
   - Storage is open to view when entering rooms/no cabinets/doors
   - Storage area(s) are cramped and dark
   - Temperatures and/or humidity have damaged stored items
   - Pests have damaged possessions
   - Quantity stored for each (any) season is excessive
   - Other:

____

____

2. Because He created the seasons for me to enjoy, my prayer for God's customized solution to storage problems is as follows:

____

____

____

3. The Scripture that is encouraging me to organize these storage areas *(and the courage to crawl around the attic and basement)* is the following:

____

____

____

4. In order to complete my prioritized tasks, the supplies that I will need are the following:
   - Three containers for Trash, Donate, Save
   -
   -
   -
   -

(This is a good time to read and follow "It's Time to Organize That Attic, Basement and Seasonal Storage.")

5. (*To be completed as each section is completed—Attic, Basement, Seasonal Storage*)
   I see that God helped me accomplish organizing these areas. My feelings now about these areas are:

   - Attic (include the date):

____

____

   - Basement (include the date):

____

____

- Seasonal Storage (include the date):

- My *one year later* journal entry about these rooms is (include the date):

It's Time to Organize That

Basement/Attic/Seasonal Storage

I have met clients who could open their own discount store merely by offering their abundance of holiday decorations for resale! This does not include their seasonal storage items of which they must have *everything* for the deck, the beach, the ski resort, the spring planting season, and Halloween. We just have too much! It is time to take control.

The goal here will be to *sort and label* by season, *purging* as we go. So we need those three containers again: Save, Donate, and Trash. Here we go!

Holiday and Seasonally Decorative Items

If you do not have items already sorted by holidays or season, this is the *first step.* Place Christmas, Halloween, fall, Easter, summer, etc. items in separate piles.

Once all items are sorted by the holiday or season, begin to sort by *need.* This is the result of asking oneself, "Do I really need to keep this?" Hopefully, the answer will be resoundingly, "No!" Purging all of the separated piles of unnecessary items, evaluate the amount left to store. This reminds me of an enormous holiday storage problem that I encountered, and I want to share my solution with you.

A PERSONAL ORGANIZING STORY

Collections of Christmas decorations can be overwhelming for many reasons. First, we collect all the cute ornaments that our children make throughout their school years. Second, we tend to overbuy after Christmas when prices are 50 percent off. Third, Christmas decorations can become memorabilia in their own respect, making it difficult to discard anything.

This happened to me. We had two wonderful mothers and one "adopted" grandmother. When they died, I "inherited" all of the Christmas tree trimmings. Each ornament and tiny decoration held sweet memories. Remember that strand of beads, large outdoor lights, and seven ornaments that belonged to my in-laws? Well, they became mine, along with several boxes of beautiful ornaments from these three mothers. Adding to the bounty, I had dutifully saved those precious grade school ornaments our children had made. In good conscience, I could not give them to Goodwill or sell them at a garage sale. But how can anyone preserve the memories yet limit the quantity and space needed to store these? Would it be greedy to keep them all and not share them with my married children? How could I solve this dilemma: clear my storage room of clutter, share them with family, and yet be free to "move on" to create my own Christmas memorabilia?

I began a *thankful and prayerful* sorting as I identified each mother's and then each child's ornaments. God had blessed us with many happy Christmas memories with these moms and young children opening treasures together. Soon I was surrounded by piles of beautiful, sparkling glass baubles and egg carton ornaments. The circle around me gave me the idea for a wreath–a memory wreath. These memories could be attached to wreaths and kept for years. I dispersed the ornaments into 4 piles, one for each of my three grown, married children and one for myself. The plan was coming together.

I purchased four large, imitation Christmas wreaths

and proceeded to attach these ornaments with hot glue. Seeing space still available, I decided to take this "memory wreath" a step further by attaching old skeleton keys from our farmhouse, buttons from dresses I had worn on our honeymoon, pine cones from the large trees on our farm, dried babies' breath from tired floral arrangements. Next, I evaluated our children's handmade ornaments. I made sure they got their originals back, and then when able, I divided them into the other children's wreaths. This way they had something made by their siblings as well as the items from the grandmothers.

Giving these to them that Christmas was a wondrous event in itself. They sat analyzing each ornament and sharing memories of the Christmases at grandmothers' homes. Not only were they amazed at the ornaments, they were amazed that their mother had held onto anything from her honeymoon! These "memory wreaths" now are displayed each Christmas season in all of our homes above mantels and in hallways to remind all of us of the wonderful gift God gave us in our heritage. I was reminded again how God answers our prayers and is interested in our lives, even in the preserving of childhood memories.

If you do not already have them, purchase new, covered storage bins. No matter where you store holiday or seasonally decorative items, they should be moisture, rodent, and dust resistant. Pay close attention to the climate or temperature of the area you will be storing these items. For instance, you would not want to store candles in the attic. You will not want to store paper items or memorabilia in a basement that has a water problem. You get the picture.

Also to be considered is their *accessibility.* Do not

stack containers too high; they will be hard to reach or they can tumble unexpectedly. Do not store them in an area that is cramped and hard to access carrying your containers, such as in the narrowest part of a basement stairwell. Also, provide some sort of light in your storage area. It will make storing and accessing much easier. *Place the current storage containers in the back.* The next holiday or season will not be the one you are now placing in storage. Your current storage container will not be needed for one year. A constant rotation will occur as you always place the current storage containers to the back. It will be worth the effort. Using this method, those needed containers will be right in front at the next season.

Labeling

Here is where you can be practical and creative at the same time. I have seen many methods and they work well. The idea is to be consistent. I suggest whatever method you choose, put a *large* label on *each end* of the container. That way the description of contents will always be visible. Here are some suggestions:

Post-Its: These handy notes now come in a large size. These are excellent and easily replaced.

Computer Labels: These can be generated on your computer and look very "organized," perhaps even official. These labels can be purchased in larger sizes, and remember to keep your font size large so it can be read at a distance. On a lower label, you could provide a detailed list if you feel it will help you later.

Handwritten Labels: Again, use those large, stick-on labels for the computer. But use your best penmanship and a dark, permanent marker. Be sure to print large enough to read it at a distance. Perhaps you would want to add a splash of color or artwork here to make identification easier at a glance. Some people add colored bands using their markers; for instance, green and red stripes on the label to mark Christmas decorations, etc.

Colored Paper: Some people really respond to colors. Do you? If so, you may find it fun and time-saving to just put orange paper (for pumpkins) on the fall boxes, red on Christmas boxes, green (for leaves) on spring boxes, blue (for water) on summer boxes, and so forth. Perhaps the Christmas boxes would benefit from a detailed list under this color since it is great to know if you are pulling out a box of ornaments or table decorations. This method is really easy to see what boxes are for what season at a quick glance. This method also saves you the expense of buying those specially colored containers at seasonal prices since your colored paper will indicate the season on each box.

Seasonal/Special Use Storage

Unlike the seasonally decorative items, this storage will take more space because so much of this is *bulky and hard to store.* Items for this may fall into several categories: hunting equipment, camping gear, perishable deck furnishings, summer sports equipment, special cooking and serving pieces to use at parties, etc. Whatever your lifestyle, you need some extra items that do not fit with the rest of your household and are needed only at different seasons or specific events. Here are some suggestions in how to store them.

Shelving: Purchasing special shelving for these items

always seems to be the easiest answer. It will keep it in view, keep it at eye level and be easily accessed. However, consider the dust and/or mold factors here. If you have coffee pots, serving trays, or toasters, you do not want dust sifting into the crevices. If things are kept on a shelf, try to contain them in a clear, zippered bag or tote/bin to eliminate dust and see the item clearly. The new, large size zipper bags or recycling comforter or bedding bags will work really well.

Cabinet with doors: A better option than shelving is cabinets with doors. By putting labels on the outside of the doors, you can readily find what is inside. Dust is not as much a factor with these.

Be creative! I already told you that I am quite "frugal," and new shelving or cabinets were just not in my budget. Also, they would have robbed me of much needed floor space in my storage/furnace room. Here is the idea we used:

A PERSONAL ORGANIZING STORY

Eight large camper cushions, sleeping bags, camper blankets and pillows, four fluffy deck chair cushions, a fabric deck table umbrella, a cotton gazebo cover, and the hammock "webbing" were my worst challenges for mice and bug free storage. When stacked, they consumed an area of about five feet long by four feet high. These were all large but not terribly heavy. Actually, they took about the space of a twin bed, but we had no room in our spare bedroom to share with these cumbersome objects.

As I wandered through the house, I began prayerfully asking God to reveal a good space yet keep this out of sight. Opening the door to our furnace room, the only space was up high. We both looked at the space in the corner above our water softener unit and water tanks, but with plenty of clearance to the floor above.

Not wanting to make this a building project, we came up with an old door that was about the right dimensions to hold these in a "loft." We purchased four large, screw-in hooks (these are usually used in garages) and several feet of sturdy chain. After screwing the hooks into the floor beams overhead, we hooked the chains at the correct length to form a "U" to hold each end of the old door. After laying the door on the chains, we could adjust the chains up or down. This gave us a sturdy, yet flexible "loft shelf" on which we began placing all the above items, flattest on the bottom and so forth. Many items are stored in plastic bags, and all of it is ready for use and can be easily accessed each summer season. I am so thankful God is a God of *vision.* He proved again that He will help preserve the blessings He has given us and that we don't always need more, we just need to use what we have.

Can such a "loft" work for you? The saying "Think outside the box," applies here. Shelving would not have worked for me. Cabinets would not have worked. I needed a large area to store large items. Perhaps you can use some attic space above a garage or an unused, empty closet for this type of storage. *Just be sure the area is clean and pest-free and climate controlled.*

Now that you have sorted, purged, and reorganized the basement, attic, and extra storage areas, walk through each, making a list of what items are stored in each area. Keep this list in your newly organized files under "Storage Areas." It's time to finish by giving God the praise for these accomplishments.

Give Credit to the Lord

Dear God of all creation, I am so thankful today for the spaces You have given me. I am thankful for all the items You have directed me to save and look with excitement toward the next holiday and season when I can find what I need without frustration or loss. Remind me as I transform my home with each season that You are in the business of transforming me. Give me the strength to be firm in my commitment that I will follow You. Thank You for Your holy Word and the truth it has shown me. It is suspending me above this world. I pray in the name of Jesus. Amen.

Now go back a few pages and complete *My Attic/Basement/Seasonal Storage Journal.*

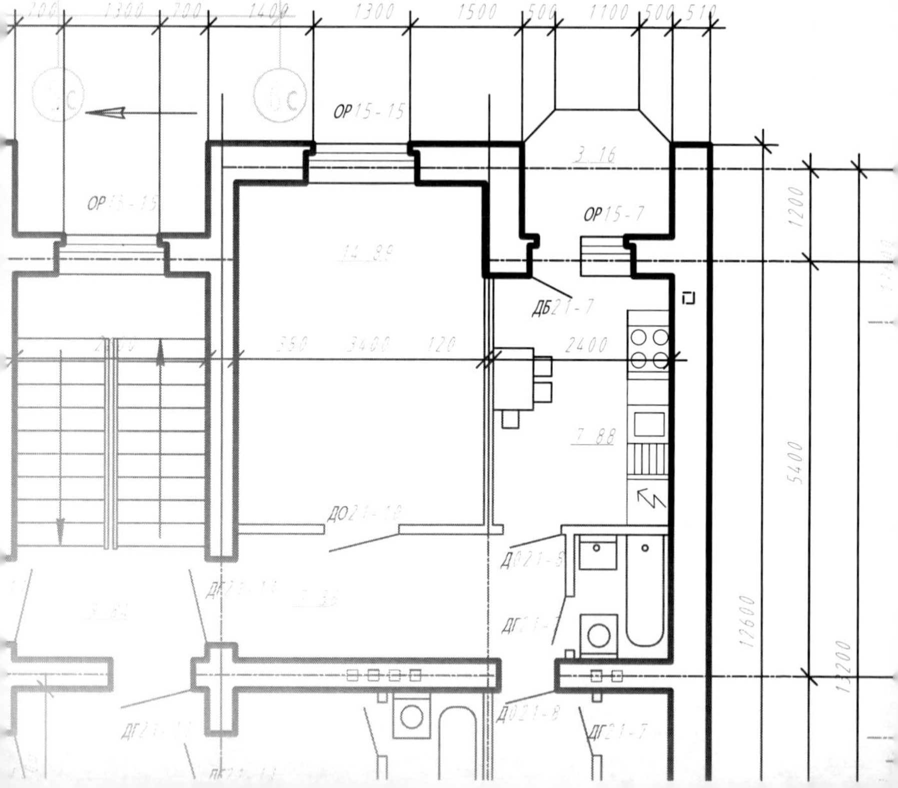

700
1300
700
1400
1300
1500
500
1100
500
510
ОР15-15
ОР15-15
3.16
ОР15-7
14.89
ДБ21-7
360
3400
120
2400
7.88
ДО21-10
ДО21-8
1200
5400
12600
13200
ДО21-8
ДГ21-7

(S)Tow Away Zone

The Garage

Being the first area strangers see as they approach our home or drive by, we want to send a message that we do not live in the same chaos behind the inner doors of our homes as our garage appears. I have visited many homes where the interior is immaculate, but the garage is so full the cars sit in the driveway. Many of us shove all the clutter out into the garage and decide to live with it. We just can't deal with it. Because our families have many diverse interests and needs, the garage becomes the catch-all for everyone's personal junk.

How can we solve this? Where will we go with it all? How can we get every family member to continue this organization once the job is finished? The answers lie in the *easy access* of necessary items while intentionally keeping a neat, orderly appearance in the garage. As much as everyone will enjoy the eye-appeal of an organized garage, they will love finding their equipment even more.

Are you ready to go? Start those cars, move them out, and let's start cleaning that garage. But first, let's stop and ask the Lord to give us direction in sorting, safety, and storage.

Oh, dear God, how blessed I am to have an entire room to store our car and all the items that make our family what it is. You know this is the last room I see each day as I leave and the first room to greet me when I return home at night. I need to be greeted by order. I need You to give me great imagination and wisdom as I clean and organize this garage. Please touch my heart with Your Word as I study it. I am expecting a blessing from You as I do this project. Amen.

N-Ice Job!

Car Areas

Come and see what God has done, how awesome his works in man's behalf! He turned the sea into dry land, they passed through the waters on foot—come, let us rejoice in him. He rules forever by his power, his eyes watch the nations—let not the rebellious rise up against him. Praise our God, O peoples, let the sound of his praise be heard; he has preserved our lives and kept our feet from slipping.

—Psalm 66: 5–9, NIV, Scofield Study Bible

"Dashing through the snow" has a personal meaning in Michigan. The gift given by our January driving is salt, sand, and slush dropping off the cars in our garages. Depending on the temperatures, this mixture ranges from frozen piles to oozing rivers sloping to the drains. Either way, it all begins to track into the house as we walk from the cars to the kitchen.

Enter the Dutch housewife, namely yours truly. It's a bright, sunny, blue sky day with a balmy four degree Fahrenheit temperature. Exit the helpful husband on an errand to the store. The garage is almost empty, except for those slush piles and muddy shoe prints. Grabbing the hose that is hooked to warm water in the garage, I sprayed off all the slush, chasing it out of the doorway into the yard. The floor looks like a pond. The drain must be frozen. A large push broom whooshes those puddles out the door and down the drive. I did notice the floor felt a bit "greasy," but it was clean, clean, clean!

No sooner had I hung up my push broom than the "errand boy" returned. As he started to get out of the car, I noticed an arm flying above the roof of the car, then heard a thud. I was wondering why he was inspecting the undercarriage of the car when I realized I was "skating on thin ice"—in more ways than one. That "greasy" feeling had turned to a skim of ice on the cement floor. There we were, in the middle of my newly formed ice rink, twenty feet from safety and sanity without any ice skates. Holding onto the car frame, the walls, the garbage can, the steps, and then the door, we made our way gingerly back inside.

How could I make amends for sending my unsuspecting husband sliding like a hockey puck? Knowing he loved sunshine, I grabbed a brand new (cheap!) chaise-lounge camping chair and set it in front of our window and under the skylight. The bright January day just beamed into the house. Getting him a fresh cup of coffee, I coaxed him to come and lie down in this little spot of sunshine. No sooner had he closed his eyes when the entire chair collapsed, leaving him flat on the floor. Slowly he rolled over, got up, and asked if I was trying to kill him. He has since told all of our children and friends that if anything strange happens to him that they must check me out. He should know I'd never seriously do that. Who would I have to torture if he weren't around?

That cold, January day is just a memory now, an unintentionally funny memory. It is also one that can serve to remind me of God's great care of us. Though it was comical to watch, my husband could have been seriously injured by just one of my good intentions. God surely protected him from hitting his head on the cement or breaking a bone or his back on the collapsing chair. How often do we take time to recount God's great care of us? At a time when it is so easy to complain about life, take a moment to go back to those memories in your life when you know God was intervening for you. I could go on for hours, but here are a few of mine:

A bike accident in my youth resulted in only damaged teeth instead of a head injury; our oldest son's third degree burns on his hand resulting in only scars and no impairments; our daughter's fall down an open cistern full of large shards of glass, and she did not have even one scratch on her; our other son's eight-foot fall resulted in a cut on his neck instead of a broken neck, paralysis, or death; my husband's fall from a roof (twice!) with only broken ribs and nothing more serious; our first grandchild's death took her to Heaven where she is awaiting us to join her; our second grandchild's fight with cancer and her complete healing; the miracle of each birth of our children and grandchildren; the blessing of food on my table; the blessing of this day called "Today." The list is endless with praises for *monumental* provisions down to having something as seemingly insignificant as our toothbrush.

In the Psalms, the Israelites recounted God's protection and provision for them. They considered all that He had done for them and praised Him and thanked Him. Can we do any less? We may not have been freed from slavery, but He has provided jobs and an income for us. God may not have parted any water for us lately, but He certainly made a safe way for us to get to our job and home again. He did not gush water out of a rock, but He did give us safe drinking water and food to eat. He promises to help protect us from temptation and evil. Let's not take anything for granted. He has protected and He has provided. He has kept our feet from slipping!

Thinking back, God, I realize I have not given You the praise and thanks that You deserve. I realize again Your holiness, Your complete protection, and Your complete provision for me. When I think of it, I am unworthy to even whisper Your name; You are so holy. Thank You so much for Jesus Who has made the way for me to come to You in praise and thanksgiving. Review in my mind today all the times You have been holding on to me and helping me. I praise and thank You for the awareness of Your holy presence. I pray in Christ's Name. Amen.

"This is the true joy in life, the being used for a purpose recognized by yourself as a mighty one; the being thoroughly worn out before you are thrown on the scrap heap; the being a force of nature instead of a feverish selfish little clod of ailments and grievances complaining that the world will not devote itself to making you happy."[11]

John Ortberg

Drill 'N Fill

Tools

For I know the plans that I have for you, declares the Lord, plans to prosper you and not to harm you, plans to give you hope and a future.

—Jeremiah 29:11, NIV, Scofield Study Bible

Is it me, or is it hot in here? As I've aged, temperatures have become more important to me. That was reason enough to want a new indoor/outdoor thermometer.

Being handy with a drill, this was a perfect job for my husband. He thought he would surprise me by installing it while I was at work. After drilling the hole at just the right spot from the inside and pushing the wire sensor to the outside, he went out to fill the hole. Using a caulking gun, he wanted to fill that hole so cold air and bugs couldn't get inside. Inserting the caulking tube, he pumped and pumped, but the hole never seemed to feel full. Climbing down from the ladder, he went back inside. There in the middle of the room was a pile of sticky, white caulking the size of a small dog on our new hunter green carpeting. The gun had just shot the caulking straight through the wall in a colossal stream of goop. Scraping it up, cleaning the carpet, and disposing of the evidence took the rest of his morning.

In disgust, he went to the garage and removed the large drill bit from the drill. Giving it a toss into a basket of tools, he walked away, ready to eat lunch. A slow, hissing noise caught his attention. It was coming from the basket of tools. Bending over to check it out, the hissing went from slow to bursting as his face came near. Suddenly, his face, shirt, and hands were being misted with a tar-based tree pruning spray. The flying drill bit had punctured the can creating this black cloud of tar. By the time he found a rag to cover it, the spray was all over the basket, the tools, the floor, and my husband.

The only solvent he found to get it off his skin was gasoline. Now his skin was irritated. He raced to the shower, scrubbing and rinsing until he was raw. *Ah-h-h-h-h.* Relief. What a day it had already been. Looking back as he exited the shower, he found tar footprints all over the white bathtub and on the carpet. After scouring the tub with more gasoline, he washed up and at 2:00 p.m. put on his pajamas and swore to do nothing else for the rest of the day. I found him slumped in his chair, ready for bed at 5:30 p.m. My laughter at his recounting of his day certainly didn't help his mood. I told him it was better than most sitcoms we have seen! But he did end up laughing with me as we went to check out the thermometer. And I was right. It *was* hot in there.

Calamities come in several forms. On that particular day, my husband seemed to move from one mess to another, and each got worse than the previous one. We all seem to have days like that at one time or another. We easily call them "bad days." Aren't so many of our "bad days" really not so bad after all? Yes, they're inconvenient, aggravating, or annoying, but they're really not "*bad.*" A really bad day is when you learn you or a loved one has a terminal illness or you find your child has made a bad decision that will cause them and you untold grief or someone you love dies and their presence is lost for many years or any other major difficult event that brings a life change.

But God has promised "tears into joy," "songs in the night," and "a heart that is merry." May we have the discernment to know the difference, the sense of humor to see ourselves from God's perspective, and the strength not to complain or become downhearted by annoying, daily circumstances. God's plan is to prosper us by giving us *hope.* That hope is the assurance of our secure future with Him, *forever.*

My dearest Lord, I am asking You for perspective today. Help me to keep a good sense of humor about little, annoying events and be sensitive to the needs of those around me who really need my care and love. I know that You are encouraging me to view the hope You have given me. Thank You for having a plan for me, a plan that will bring no harm to me. I know my future is assured in You because You are my Savior. I pray in the name of Jesus. Amen.

Mouse with a Sole

Pests

His eyes are on the ways of men; He sees their every step. There is no dark place, no deep shadow, where evil doers can hide.

—Job 34:21–22, NIV, New Scofield Study Bible

As the temperatures drop, mice look for warm winter homes, like mine. I've always hated mice. They represent everything nasty that lives outdoors and has no place coming indoors.

Years ago, during an average evening meal, we heard a slight rattling of jars in the pantry off the kitchen. Quiet. We all listened. There it was again, jars moving and bumping just enough to hear. A hush fell over the children. Daddy rose from his chair and silently stalked over to the cabinets. Their confidence in Daddy, the hunter/protector, was being reinforced. Daddy heard one more rattle and threw open the pantry door. The small, brown mouse literally flew through the air to the floor and began running here and there to escape him. The cheerleaders at the table were waving their forks like pom-poms. They encouraged his frenzied steps as he tried to outsmart that mouse by yelling, "Get him, Daddy! Get him, Daddy!" Clomp, stomp, jump, stomp. Then, as suddenly as it began, the stomping stopped. *Ew-w-w-w-w.* Daddy had caught the mouse. Cleaning his shoe and calming his nauseous fans, Daddy came back to the dinner table. Somehow, everyone had lost their appetite. Why couldn't we be like other families and just get a cat?

Dark corners, garages, basements, pantries, under the sink, that's where mice love to find a place to hide. They chew on our valuables until they have enough "fluff" to make a warm nest and then proceed to have litters of dozens of more mice. I am speaking from experience. Those hidden nests have sheltered the masses that have invaded our home every fall season.

God sees into every dark place in our lives and into the dark places of the world. I wonder what He thinks. I cannot imagine how sickened He is when He sees man's cruelty to other men in countries where people are punished or killed for being a Christian. How does He feel every time someone murders or robs someone else? How does He keep from handing out punishment when children are abused? How does He still love all of mankind in spite of all that we do?

That love is too vast, too patient for us to begin to understand. While we think God should chase evil down and squash it like that little nasty mouse, He has a different plan. We don't understand this plan, but we know that in the future He will put a final stop to all the evil in this world with the return of His holy son, Jesus.

Are you ready? Are you living in a dark place, hiding from God? Why not come into His light today and ask Jesus to be your Savior? Tell him that you believe that Jesus came and gave His life, taking the punishment for all the bad things you have ever done. There is no way to hide anything from the all-seeing eyes of our holy God.

If you have already asked Jesus to be your Savior, how are you living? Are you hiding secrets in dark places for fear someone will find out how you really live? Are you living in the garage or out in the light, near the "window"? He sees your every step, He knows your actions. Commit today to climb the stairs out of those dark places by confessing your sin and choosing to walk out into the light: God's forgiving light.

Dear holy God, I believe that Jesus is Your son and that He paid the penalty for my sin with His death on the cross. I believe that He did not stay dead, but is alive now, making a home for me in heaven. I have done so many wrong things, and I ask You for Your forgiveness today. Please move me from that dark place of having no hope to Your light by opening my mind to these truths. I know You see my every step, and I want them to be in the right direction. Thank You for Jesus. Thank You for hope. Thank You for my future with You. I pray in the name of my living Savior, Jesus Christ. Amen.

My Garage Journal

"I promise to work on this room and not take on the organization of any other room until my garage is in proper order."

1. Circle or name three major problem areas in your garage, prioritizing them with numbers.

   - Walkways are crowded and dangerous
   - Sports equipment and/or toys are hard to access
   - Tools are dangerously exposed
   - Tools are hard to reach
   - Boxes are everywhere
   - Cars are parked outside due to clutter
   - Insects and rodents frequently damage our possessions
   - Chemicals and poisons are not safely stored
   - Temperatures in the garage have ruined items
   - Other:

____

____

2. Besides knowing God has blessed me with a car, tools, and many other enjoyable items, I also know He wants me to care for them. My prayer for His customized solution is the following:

____

____

____

3. The Scripture that has encouraged me to organize this garage is the following:

____

____

____

4. In order to complete my prioritized tasks, I will need the following supplies:
   - Three containers for Trash, Donate, Save
   -
   -
   -
   -

(This is a good time to read and follow "It's Time to Organize That Garage.")

5. (*To be completed after the garage organization is finished*) I see that God cares even about my garage. My feelings about this now are (include today's date):

____

____

____

6. My *one year later* journal entry about this garage is (include the date):

____

____

____

It's Time to Organize That

Garage

This will be the last room you see driving out in the morning and the first room to greet you in the evening. Do you want to leave and arrive with a feeling of chaos or with a feeling of order? This room can settle you back into the mood that you are entering your place of refuge, control, and peace. Or you can trip over bicycles and kick the dog. This will be one organizing job that will pay big dividends each time you drive in and out.

The organization of the garage will consist of: sorting, safety, and storage. I would recommend returning to the "Circular Organization" pattern for sorting your garage. That is, start in one corner, preferably near one door, and work in a circle around to the other side. In order to sort, get those three containers ready: "Trash," "Donate," and "Save." Gentlemen, start your engines … and move them out and away from the garage.

Sorting

We will be emptying the entire garage, sorting as we go. The sorting will be done into "like" piles. There will probably be piles for tools, sports equipment, car maintenance, paint, garden equipment, gasoline and other chemicals, recyclable items, bikes, and possibly, toys. These would be some of the common items in a garage, but yours may reflect a special need or interest. Whatever you do, *group items according to use.*

As you are going through the piles, be sure to *be constantly purging by donating or throwing away unused items* to reduce the quantity you are deciding to keep.

After the entire garage is emptied and items are in piles (boxes would help store temporarily), this is a good time to evaluate the interior of your garage. Take a look at the walls. If you do not already have it, would you prefer a finished look? Paneling or new drywall could be hung before going too much further.

As you are in the evaluative mode, be aware that there are some wonderful new "garage systems" available at your local home improvement stores. These would make your storage arrangement much easier and would also add a finished look to the walls. This is the stage to do your homework and purchase what you need to make that garage look the way you want it to.

Once you have sorted everything and decided on the interior look of this space, it is time for the next step: safety.

Safety

Several factors need to be considered here depending on the items you intend to store in your garage. I will touch on some of the common ones, but you must be the last authority on the safety of everyone in your household.

Chemicals/Poisons

Everything that has a warning label on the container has to be taken seriously. Remember, you are not the only one entering or using the garage. The best rule for anything poisonous is to place it up high, and if young children are in the home, put a lock on the storage unit.

These questionable chemicals can range from bug sprays to automotive additives, paint solvents, mouse poisons, gasoline for power equipment, and cleaning solvents. If you are not able to find a way to store them in a high area with their same groups, then select one storage unit to keep locked at all times for safety purposes.

In our colder climate, we must also consider the freezing factor. Most paints cannot be used after freezing. It destroys the composition. Consider taking paints to a safe storage inside the house during cold, winter months.

Gasoline must be stored in marked containers and kept out of contact with sparks and heat.

Replace all protective caps on spray cans, and tighten all caps so children cannot get them open.

If you are *disposing of any solvents or poisonous chemical,* call your local poison prevention hotline for their recommendations. You may also find your local fire department helpful in this. *Do not* pour old chemicals onto the ground, place them in your garbage, or try to dispose of them without professional advice.

Power and Sharp Tools

Just like that drill bit my husband tossed into the basket, so many of the tools we use are sharp and dangerous. As you evaluate the use of each tool, consider the risks of grabbing or bumping these and how to place the sharp edges or points for safety.

If you lack the professional storage containers for sharp items such as drill bits, knives, small garden tools, etc., you can use a jar or small bucket, aiming the points into the bottom with handles exposed. Hatchets, saw blades, *anything sharp* needs to be hung up high or kept in a closed cabinet.

After considering the potential poisons and sharp

objects, the next safety issue would be walkways and space.

Walkways

This is mentioned because you may have just emptied out a garage that you could barely walk through, if at all. Unless you have done a good job of purging, you will soon find yourself in much the same situation as before you began this project. Safe walkways in your garage are just as important as putting the poisons out of reach. Bumping into wheelbarrows, tripping over hoses or cords can be just as dangerous. Make a decision at this point how much space is needed to *walk safely* between the cars, around the cars, and in front of the cars. You don't even need ice on your floor to cause a slip-and-fall when it is so crowded that your clothing catches on the car mirrors and pulls you down. If you need to, mark with sidewalk chalk (I love that stuff!) where your boundaries will be for walking areas in your garage. By doing this, you will have a good idea of what size units to buy for your designated storage areas, the next phase of organizing your garage.

Storage Spaces

Well, you got the entire garage sorted, you have taken steps for safety with tools and chemicals, you have drawn a chalk outline of the new walkways, and you are ready to buy storage units. Now the fun begins. Measure first! There are so many storage units out there that you may feel completely overwhelmed at first. Measure! Be sure to measure wall spaces as well as your floor space. Wall units or hanging systems can double your available storage. Here is a dynamic suggestion: *Take it slow (Measure!)* Buy units for only one area at a time. Whatever you decide to buy (after measuring), try to contain it behind doors to make your garage look neat at all times. Did I mention that you should *measure* the space needed for every unit you buy? I cannot emphasize that enough! Take your measurements as well as that tape measure to the store to match up the best storage container(s) for each need.

Sports equipment, bikes, and toys: The kids may not have the patience to wait for you to organize the entire garage before they can get back at their fun, so make their toys and fun a priority. Get a bike rack(s) that is a space saver. Have you seen the wall-mounted or ceiling-mounted racks? Get a large toy bin for young children's outdoor toys that can later be used to store deck items. There are several new specific storage units for sports equipment. They can be wall mounted and kept near the door where the children or your golfer-husband can access them easily. Try some imagination. A large, deep shelf above the garage door would be hidden from view yet would hold large bins or objects. Use every available inch of wall space.

A PERSONAL ORGANIZING STORY

Prayer *is* the key to organizing chaos and sometimes that prayer is uttered a long time before the action or organizing begins. As a mom, we all pray for our children. My children were no exception. I prayed for them for everything from illnesses to mates to finances to pets and even to be able to run efficient, fun homes for their families when they were grown. They have all survived many illnesses, have wonderful mates, are financially independent, have had their share of good (and bad) pets, and all have established efficient and even fun homes for their families. What a blessing to see God answer all those prayers of all those years.

One of our sons recently demonstrated his efficiency when the house was overrun with balls. Basketballs, volleyballs, soccer balls, cheap grocery store balls, baseballs, softballs, and tennis balls; there were just too many balls at his house. Using a drill, he mounted short dowels at a slight angle on a board and spaced them so each type of ball was securely supported. Next, he hung this board-of-balls up at the right height for the children. By recycling materials he had on hand and limiting the space this rack would take, he created an inexpensive yet really helpful storage area for this "roly-poly" collection. Within just an hour or so, all the balls were contained, easy to reach, and kept clean, out from underfoot. It doesn't need to be an expensive organizing unit, just practical. Isn't it amazing how God keeps on answering? Good job!

Tools: If your husband is a real handyman, you will want to look at some of the storage units that will create a small bench, some specific hangers for small and power tools and a cabinet of some sort. Local home improvement stores are the best resource for these units. If he is not a handyman, you still need basic tools, and the longer you own a home, the more you seem to accumulate. Put these in smaller, clear storage bins on shelves in your new storage units. If you can, get specific racks for screw drivers, a hammer and some automotive tools.

As well as tools, extension cords are always needed in the garage. But they tend to tangle and are hard to store. Purchasing a wall-mounted reel-type extension cord is a great help. This allows easy access, no tangling, and prevents cords laying on the floor when not in use.

Automotive: Do-it-yourselfers on auto repairs seem to be extinct. Most of us go to auto service centers for oil changes and mechanical work, but we still need some basic items. Car washing soap, windshield cleaner, bug remover, leather cleaner, that extra can of oil, etc. can all be contained on a shelf in your new storage cabinets.

Garden equipment: Just like the quantities of tools for the husband/handyman, the amount of gardening equipment you need to store will depend if you plant a quarter acre or only water the hanging pot you buy at the greenhouse. A small, rolling potting bench can hold most of the tools and equipment plus be taken closer to your plants as needed. Roll up hoses or hose reels can eliminate a lot of wasted space. Hanging a wheelbarrow on the wall and a corner or a wall-mounted rack for garden tools (rakes, shovels, etc.) will give you more floor space. If you mow your own lawn, you need space for a mower. Perhaps one of the *outdoor* storage units for this and the gasoline would be a good investment. Whatever route you take, *keep it uncluttered, handy, and safe.*

Miscellaneous: Life is miscellaneous! Every garage needs a bit of space for something that just cannot go in the house but needs a "home." Allow for hobbies, fun creative projects, or just something that you cannot throw out, just yet.

Keeping all of it behind doors will give you a clean, uncluttered feeling. Use a label-maker, and *put labels on each door* so everyone can begin to remember where their belongings are stored. After a while, they will know where to look. It will become like the kitchen cupboards. They don't throw their dishes or glasses on the floor in the kitchen, do they? They know which cupboard and which shelf where each dish or glass belongs, so they put it there. The garage will become the same in time.

Having completed the last "room" in the house, we need to take time to praise the Lord for all He has done helping us through this.

Give Credit to the Lord

Dearest God, how can I thank You enough for helping me organize this chaotic garage? Please help each member of my family to realize their lives are better because of all that You have helped us do in this last "room" of our home. We seek peace and joyful living, and the organization of this messy garage will help us. Please help me to use each tool wisely for You and to find joy in recreation because our equipment can be found. Lord, as I move through it each day, help me to remember that we are preventing accidents and injuries because of this careful storage. I know this garage is important to Your plan because so much of our lives happen here. We leave to enter the "mission field" every day from here, and we return looking forward to the reuniting of our family in the evenings. Never let me think any room or any person is insignificant to You. Thank You for Your loving care and patience with me. In Christ's name, I pray. Amen.

Now go back a few pages and complete *My Garage Journal*

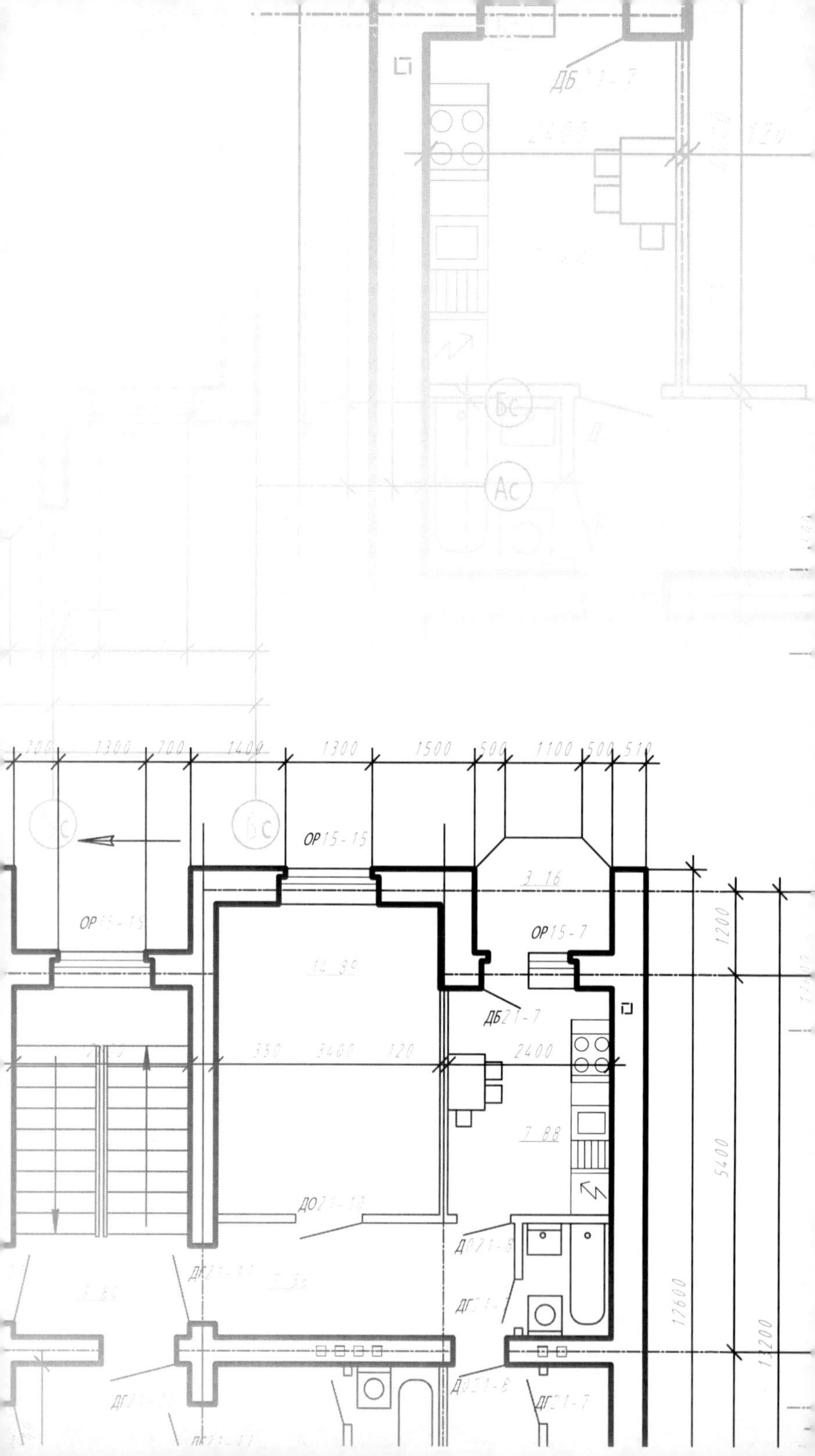

ДБ21-7
Бс
Ас
200
1300
700
1400
1300
1500
500
1100
500
510
ОР15-15
ОР15-15
3.16
ОР15-7
14.39
ДБ21-7
330
3400
120
2400
1200
7.88
5400
ДО21-13
ДО21-8
ДГ21-7
12600
13200
ДО21-8
ДГ21-7

Epilogue

You've done it! You've reached the final destination of an organized home! Mind you, I did not say you now have a "perfect" home, just one that is organized. And that has been our goal all along. No one wants to live in a sterile and perfect environment. But living in a home where you can find your belongings daily brings a calming atmosphere to you and your family.

Maintenance. Wow! It will be so much easier to be in a continual mode of sorting and storing everything in its proper place that maintenance will be much easier than you thought. Just don't let it get ahead of you. Encourage and engage your family in this task on a daily and weekly basis. It should only take a few minutes each day to do general grooming of all areas. Frequently, set aside some time to do a deep sorting and cleaning and you will find you will be able to maintain an organized home.

And what role did you find that *prayer* had in your

organizational efforts? As you studied God's Word and prayed over each room, I hope you found a *release* from ownership of the unnecessary, *courage* to part with it, and *gratitude* to the Lord for all He has given you. New eyes are given to us as we see God in every aspect of our lives. We spend the majority of our time in our homes, and that is where we need to see Him helping us and blessing us.

As I draw these remarks to a close, a sad reminder unfolds right outside my window. A dear neighbor passed away recently. The children's cars and trucks have been gathering for several days, loading and unloading her stuff. Today, the typical dumpster appeared in the yard, and family members will begin to fill it with the remains of her stuff.

That "stuff" *we* are holding onto will all be in dumpsters someday, possibly placed there by someone we thought would care. There is a simple truth here: the only possessions we leave that will have value to others are our time, our photos, family heirloom memorabilia, and exquisitely expensive items. The rest will be just stuff: dumpster filler.

I do not add these views to make you sad, but to inspire you by taking a painfully realistic look at the result of not bringing order and control to your possessions, your time, and your finances. You will leave a burden to the next generation. Your "valuables" will likely only have value to you, and the next generation will purge your house if you don't do it.

Our legacy should be one of time well spent with those we love, a good reputation of financial responsibility, living memorably, and "living leanly." Lean living brings a freedom from the accumulation of "stuff" and a motivation to spend each moment wisely. In this entire legacy, our commitment to Christ, a home dedicated to Him, and a life exemplifying the power of prayer will leave an indelible mark on the world around us.

Continue to pray over your home, your efforts, your stressful areas, and watch God work in your heart to give you the wisdom to deal with all of it. As you have been challenged by this entire project, remember that *God is the victor for the challenged.* Continue to bring your challenges to Him, whether they are organizational challenges or any challenge in life. He wants you to have the life of victory—His life.

Endnotes

1. Erma Bombeck. *Forever, Erma.* Andrews and McMeel, 1996.

2. Erma Bombeck. *A Marriage Made in Heaven or Too Tired for an Affair.* Harper and Collins, 1993.

3. Nancy Dorner. *A Woman's Guide to Spiritual Power through Scriptural Prayer.* Starburst Publishers, 1992.

4. Erma Bombeck. *Forever, Erma.* Andrews and McMeel, 1996.

5. Dr. Criswell Freeman. *Friends Are Forever.* Walnut Grove Press, 1998.

6. Philip Yancey. *What's So Amazing About Grace?* Participant's Guide, Zondervan, 2000.

7. Dr. Criswell Freeman. *Friends Are Forever.* Walnut Grove Press, 1998.

8. Howard Dayton. *Your Money Counts.* Copyrighted: Crown Ministries, 1996.

9. Dr. Criswell Freeman. *Friends Are Forever.* Walnut Grove Press, 1998.

10. Bruce Wilkinson. *The Prayer of Jabez.* Multnomah Publishers, Inc., 2000.

11. John Ortberg. *The Life You've Always Wanted.* Zondervan, 1997.